Interview Mastery | Cabin Crew
Personal Training Program

Interview Mastery | Cabin Crew
Personal Training Program

First Edition by
Carrie Loren

Mastery
Academy

Interview Mastery | Cabin Crew
Personal Training Program

© 2011 SpineBound Books and Carrie Loren

The right of Carrie Loren to be identified as the author of this work has been asserted in accordance with the Copyright, Design and Patents Act 1988

First Edition, 2011

ISBN 10:   1-908300-00-0
ISBN 13:   978-1-908300-00-3
Digital Edition: 978-1-908300-01-0

Publisher's Note
Every possible effort has been made to ensure that the information contained in this book is accurate at the time of going to press, and the publishers and authors cannot accept responsibility for any errors or omissions, however caused. No responsibility for loss or damage occasioned to any person acting or refraining from action, as a result of the material in this publication can be accepted by the editor , the publisher or any of the authors.

British Library Cataloguing-in-Publication Data
A CIP catalogue record for this book can be obtained from the British library

Printed in the United Kingdom
10 9 8 7 6 5 4 3 2 1

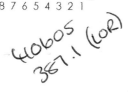

This book is available at quantity discounts for bulk purchases.
For further information, please contact:

SpineBound Books
www.SpineBound.com
Books@SpineBound.com

Written by:
Carrie Loren

Published by:

Advance Praise

"Just as Carrie Loren urges those who read her book to do their research in seeking a cabin crew position, it is apparent that she has done hers in creating and writing this thorough and thoroughly engaging book."

Joseph Yurt - Reader Views

"If you are an applicant for cabin crew, Ms. Loren presents a thorough and well articulated set of tools for you. This book is a powerful guide for a far more comprehensive set of job seekers, and I give it a very strong endorsement."

William E. Cooper - Reader Views

"Dreaming of a career in the skies? Then Carrie Loren's new guide to getting hired by the airlines is what you need, A must-have for anyone wanting to be cabin crew."

Janet White
Author of Secrets of the
Hidden Job Market

"I contacted you when I was starting out my Cabin Crew Career and at the time you gave me lots of really good advice. Since securing my first Cabin Crew Job last year with Excel Airways I've been having a fantastic time working for a Swedish Airline, Viking. I even qualified as Senior Cabin Crew earlier in the year."

Camilla Gavin

"First of all, i'd like to say thank you for the precious book and all the important information you gave every time I wrote you. I'm so happy because they called from Emirates telling I was approved to work with them. I'm going to Dubai in January. I'd like to wish you a Merry Christmas and New Year full of happiness. Thank you once more i'll be in touch. A big Hug."

Claudia Mello

"If you want to get an idea of the cabin crew interview system then buy this. I am 42 yrs old, never had a flying job before, hadnt had an interview for a job in over 10 years. I needed to know what kind of things I would be asked and what to expect. I went for 3 cabin crew jobs and got all 3 of them offered to me. Need I say more???"

Rebecca Tapsell

"The book is really amazing especially those question and answer part. Most of the answers really fits onto me while some of them serves as a correction from what i've done wrong. Its helps me in my present career as well as my personal developments. Most of them are exactly the words that describes me. I really like the content of the book. I felt like somebody interved me and turn it to a manual. More power and God Bless!"

Redentor Tuazon

Contents

Preface   vii
Quick Start Guide   xi
About the Author   xiii

Research

Part 1

The Position

The Duties   17
The Lifestyle   18
Career Path   18

The Requirements

Person Specification   19
Physical Profile   20

The Airline

Airline Selection   24
Preliminary Research   25

Prepare

Part 2

Psychological Programming

Manage your Mind Set   31
Use your Imagination   33
Anchor your State   34
Re frame your Words   36
Ask Resourceful Questions   36
Adjust your Physiology   37
Make the Swish   37
Find your Focus   39
Create Compelling Reasons   39
Affirm & Incant   39
Common Concerns   41
Three Steps to Mastery   45

Impression Management

Invent your Introduction   47
Consider your Communication   48
Create a Connection   54
Master the Art of Small Talk   56
Plan an Exit Strategy   57

Polish your Image

Organise your Outfit   59
Tend to your Grooming   62
Accessorize   62

The Final Countdown

The Run Up   63
The Evening Before   63
On the Day   64
On Arrival   65

Apply

Part 3

Write a Winning Cover Letter

Appearance   73
Conventions   74
Format   75
Going Digital   75
Prepared Phrases   76
Sample Cover Letter   78
Sample E-Cover Letter   79

Create a Compelling CV/Résumé

Appearance   81
OCR Technology   82
Format   83
Outline   84
Sample Combination Résumé   86
Going Digital   88
Sample Plain Text Résumé   89

Prepare a Powerful Application

Quick Tips   91
Guidance Notes   92
Sample Application Form   97
Going Digital   100
Action Verbs   101

Produce Polished Photographs

Requirements   103
Formal vs Informal   103
Set the Scene   103
Work the Angles   104
Dress the Part   104
Tend to your Grooming   105
Warm your Smile   106

Contents

Surpass the Telephone Screening

Format   107
Be Prepared   107
Make a Positive Impression   108
Faux Pas Alerts   110
Making a Successful Close   111

Concluding Notes

Proofread, Proofread, Proofread   113
What Happens Next?   113

Attend

Part 4

Introduction

What to Expect   119
Meet the Candidates   120
Meet the Recruitment Officers   123
Meet the Undercover Team   123

Group Activities

What Assessors Look For   125
Seven Heavenly Virtues   126
Seven Deadly Sins   127
Common Concerns   128
Points to Consider   129
Practical Tasks   131
Discussions   135
Role Play Scenarios   139

Individual Assessments

Self Introduction   141
Personality Questionnaire   142
Language Proficiency Test   142
Numerical Ability Test   144
Medical Questionnaire   144
Reach Test   144
General Knowledge Quiz   149

Panel Interview

What Assessors Look For   151
The Process   151
Seven Heavenly Virtues   152
Seven Deadly Sins   153

Q&A Survival Guide

Part 5

Competency

Introduction   159
Preparing Examples   159
The S.A.R.R Formula   160
Follow up Questions   161
Lack of Relative Experience   162

Customer Focus   163
Communication Competence   175
Team Spirit   181
Initiative and Adversity   191

Traditional

Cabin Crew   203
The Airline   208
Career History   210
Character Traits   213
Customer Focus   215
Team Spirit   217
Hypothetical   219
Adverse   222
Closing   225

Interviewing the Interviewer

Question Guidelines   227
Questions about Suitability   227
Questions about the Recruiter   228
General Questions   228
No Questions   228
Questions to Avoid   228

Conclude

Part 6

Follow Up

Sending a Thank You Letter   233
What Happens Next?   235
Coping with Setbacks   235

You're Hired!

Conditional Offer   237
Background Checks   237
Medical Examination   239
Contract of Employment   242
Ab-Initio Training   242

Disclaimer

This book is designed to provide information and guidance on attending a cabin crew assessment. It is sold with the understanding that the publisher and author are not engaged in rendering legal or other professional services. Such topics, as discussed herein are, for example, or illustrative purposes only. If expert assistance is required, the services of a competent professional should be sought where you can explore the unique aspects of your situation and can receive specific advice tailored to your circumstances.

It is not the purpose of this guide to reprint all the information that is otherwise available to candidates but instead to complement, amplify and supplement other texts. You are urged to read all the available material, learn as much as possible about the role and interview techniques and tailor the information to your individual needs.

Every effort has been made to make this guide as complete and accurate as possible. However, this guide contains information that is current only up to the printing date. Interview processes are frequently updated and are often subject to differing interpretations. Therefore, there are no absolutes and this text should be used only as a general guide and not as the ultimate source of information.

All information in this book is offered as an opinion of the author and should be taken as such and used with discretion by the reader. You are solely responsible for your use of this book. Neither the publisher nor the author explicitly or implicitly promises that readers will find employment because of anything written or implied here.

The purpose of this guide is to educate and inform. The author and Aspire Press shall have neither liability nor responsibility to you or anyone else because of any information contained in or left out of this book.

Preface

Airlines already know the secrets in this book, but are keeping them from you so they can weed out 90% of the 15,000 applications they receive monthly.

On a beautiful late spring afternoon, two young women graduated from the same college. They were very much alike, both had been better than average students, both were personable and both shared a deep desire to travel the world and enter the highly competitive and coveted profession of Airline Cabin Crew.

Recently, these women returned to college for their tenth annual reunion. They were still very much alike and both, as it turned out, had gone to work for the same Airline after graduation. But, there was a difference.

One of the women was a customer support manager, while the other was part of the elite, world travelling cabin crew team.

What Made The Difference?

Have you ever wondered, what makes this kind of difference in people's lives? It isn't a native intelligence, nor talent or dedication. It isn't that one person wants success and the other doesn't. The difference lies in what each person knows and how he or she makes use of that knowledge.

That is the whole purpose of the book: to give you knowledge — knowledge that you can use to navigate the challenging road that 90% of applicants stumble and fail on. Now you can fast-track your way, with ease, to a glamorous career with your chosen airline, that will take you to exotic countries and hotels all around the world.

Within the pages of this book, you will be given a clear and effective blueprint to follow that will take you from scratch through to hearing 'you're hired' in the shortest time possible.

You will discover essential strategies and steps that you must know in order to be successful in one of the most competitive and sought after careers in the world, and you will learn the little known-secrets that airlines use to weed out 90% of the 15,000 applications that they receive each month.

Follow the guidance, and this tell-all book is guaranteed to make sure you are in the elite 10% who are selected.

Knowledge Is Power

There are just five major areas in the hiring process, these are: Research, Prepare, Apply, Attend and Conclude. In this program, you be guided through each of these stages and discover insights into:

Research:

» Why 99% of all applicants totally miss the boat when it comes to researching an airline and the career.

Preparation:

» Three sure-fire ways to create a killer first impression

» How a simple adjustment in your mind set can give you an immediate edge over other applicants.

» Very simple tactics to prepare yourself before, on the day and when you arrive.

Applying:

» How to avoid the most common and costly application mistakes

» How to automatically avoid the blunders that get even professional photos criticized and thrown out.

» How to attract the attention of recruiters with your cover letter and resume

» The absolute best way to succeed in the telephone screening process

Attending:

» A hidden " twist " that Airlines Companies use that you must know

» The truth about what assessors are looking for in applicants

» How you can impress the "undercover team" from a mile away

» The 14 types of applicants you're up against and how to avoid the common pitfalls.

» Quick strategies to cure anxiety, solve disagreements and avoid being alienated.

» Know the most overlooked "hidden" reason why most attendees fail.

» How to use the 7 heavenly virtues to win over any panel of recruiters and the 7 deadly sins you must avoid.

» The easiest way to establish a good "chemistry" with interviewers

Question and Answers Survival Guide:

» The 31 most important competency questions they will ask and incredibly easy ways to answer them.

» How to use the concept of the S.A.R.R formula to eliminate 99% of follow-up questions

» How to never again get stumped by the toughest questions, such as: "Why should we hire you"

» Breakthrough answers for 24 of the most traditional questions asked about the job, 11 ways to answer questions about the airline and 9 quick fire examples to cover your career history

» How to triple your chances of standing out from the competition by asking the interviewer these questions

» The "no-sweat, no-brainer" way to answer any weakness and strength questions

Conclusion:

» The one simple method anybody can use to seal the deal and get hired

» What happens after you hear the words "Your Hired!"

Best of all

You will be privy to unspoken hiring practices that Airlines use, that stop even those most confident applicants from progressing through the various assessment stages. Know these, and you will slip past them without sweating a bead or batting an eye.

The Learning Process

There are four phases to the learning process, as depicted by Abraham Maslow, these are as follows:

» Phase 1: Unconscious Incompetence
In this phase, we are unaware of our own incompetence

» Phase 2: Conscious Incompetence
In this second phase, we become aware of our incompetence

» Phase 3: Conscious Competence
In the third phase, we begin to understand and practice the correct way, but it takes a conscious effort

» Phase 4: Unconscious Competence
In the fourth and final phase, we can perform the new skill effectively without any conscious thought

Three Steps to Mastery

To successfully transition through conscious competence to unconscious competence, we must follow these three steps to mastery:

» Repeat
  When we learn any new skill, we need to practice the skill many times until we can do it automatically. Studies suggest seven to twelve repetitions.

» Apply
  When we are comfortable with our grasp of the new skill, we need to apply it to our daily life.

» Reinforce
  When we have mastered the new skill, we need to keep it strong with continual use.

If you are willing to put a little time and effort into mastering the techniques in this book, you too will get the edge you need to pass the interview and live your dream - as many other readers have.

Quick Start Guide

Ideally you should allow one month or more to prepare. This will allow you ample time to study the material thoroughly, and apply the strategies without feeling too rushed.

However, it's not always the case that you will have this luxury of time. So, what's the best way to prepare when you only have a matter of weeks, or less?

Prepare your application materials
Photographs are a requirement for most airlines, so you should have these readily available. (Page 103)

Whether or not your résumé is used to apply, you should get one drafted up as it will certainly assist you when filling in your application form. (Page 81)

Read what's relevant to your circumstances
If you struggle with any element in particular, maybe your confidence holds you back or you struggle to voice your opinion in group settings, put effort into developing those areas.

Gather facts about the airline – (Page 25)
It would be a cardinal sin to arrive at the interview without having at least a basic knowledge of their operation, so do your research.

Prepare for potential questions – (Page 159-225)
At the very least, you should be prepared to answer questions such as:

» Why do you want to become cabin crew? (Page 203)

» Why do you want to work for us? (Page 208)

» Why should we hire you? (Page 205)

» What are your weaknesses? (Page 213)

You should also be prepared with examples which demonstrate your customer focus (Page 215) and team spirit (Page 217).

Rehearse
Rehearsing the interview process under simulated conditions will highlight potential areas of weakness. This will give you a better idea of where to focus your time and energy.

Prepare a list of questions - (Page 227)
Having intelligent questions prepared for the recruiters will set you apart as a prepared and enthusiastic candidate.

Prepare your outfit - (Page 59)
Presentation is the key to making a positive first impression, so prepare your outfit in advance.

Read what you can
The average reading speed is said to be 150-250 words per minute. This means that, even at the slower pace of 150 words, the whole book can be read in as little as 5-6 hours. So, if you have just a few hours to spare after you have prepared, as per the above steps, make the most of this time allocation by reading as much as you can possibly comprehend.

About the Author

Although I am now an interview coach, I too began my career as aspiring cabin crew.

From the age of 19, I spent several years going to interview after interview in pursuit of my dream. Unfortunately, I was clueless about the interview process and naive about the competition. With every rejection I experienced, my self esteem paid the price.

But I was determined to live my dream and never gave up.

Finally, after much research and preparation, I refined the process, perfected my technique and honed it down to a science. Then my pursuits began to pay off as I was hired by the largest airline in the Middle East.

Since retiring from the skies, I have turned my passion to helping others achieve the same success and, over the past six years, I have used those same techniques to coach hundreds of candidates to interview success. Now, in this ground breaking book, I will teach you those same techniques so you too can live your dream.

You already have the ability to get the job, you simply need to learn how.

Reach for the skies...

Carrie Loren

Part 1

Research

The Position
The Requirements
The Airline

The Position

The Duties

On the surface, it would appear that airline cabin crew are nothing more than glorified waiters who jet around the world, stay in luxury hotels and get paid for the privilege. In reality, the role of cabin crew is much more complex as their primary role on-board an aircraft is for safety and security reasons.

On-board an aircraft, paramedics, police and fire-fighters aren't just a phone-call away, thus the cabin crew are responsible for taking on these roles. When things go wrong, whether there is a medical emergency, a fire break-out, a terrorism threat, a violent passenger or mechanical failure, the cabin crew is there to take action. This may involve directing passengers during an evacuation, detaining an intoxicated passenger or administering first aid.

Fortunately, these types of emergency situations aren't an everyday occurrence and, during a typical flight, the cabin crew will generally spend most of their time tending to passenger comfort. While meal and beverage services play a large part of a crew's duties, their responsibilities will be as diverse as the needs of the passengers, and they generally spend much of the flight on their feet tending to those needs.

All the while, they are expected to deliver the highest standards of customer care, while appearing friendly and approachable to every passenger. As if all that wasn't enough, they must also remain calm and professional in all circumstances, regardless of the conditions.

So, to recap, here are some of the typical duties you can expect...

- » Cleaning & maintenance of cabins and galleys
- » Stock check & replenishment
- » Testing of emergency equipment
- » Overseeing the boarding and disembarking of passengers
- » Providing meal and beverage services
- » Overseeing duty-free sales
- » Completing paperwork of on-board sales and safety checks
- » Advising safety procedures and carrying out demonstrations
- » Dealing with problems or issues that arise during the flight
- » Taking charge during adverse and emergency situations

The Lifestyle

With opportunities to visit exotic destinations, meet new people and experience new cultures, the role of cabin crew does indeed appear to be a rather glamorous one.

Those who crave variety will discover a very stimulating lifestyle as the role offers variety in more ways than one. The sheer dynamics of different crew, roster structure and passenger profile mean that no two days are ever the same.

On the flip side, crew members experience flight delays and cancellations just as passengers do. The crew, however, experience these much more frequently and much of their time will be spent waiting around in airports and hotels. This makes for very long and tiring shifts, irregular working patterns and unpredictable schedules, which can be very demanding on family and social life.

In addition, jet lag may become a problem when regularly crossing different time zones which can lead to disturbed sleep patterns and fatigue. This combined with working in a confined and pressurized container with lots of time spent on your feet, continuously tending to passengers needs can be the cause of high stress levels.

Clearly the role is a very physically and mentally demanding one, but it is also a very exciting and fulfilling one for those who have the necessary qualities and are willing to put in the effort. The rewards are plenty, but the job is not for the faint of heart or those who crave routine.

Career Path

Depending on the airline, high performing cabin crew can progress on to serve the first class cabins, then onto a senior crew member and, potentially, a purser. There are even opportunities to become cabin crew trainers or recruitment personnel.

Note

Around 75 - 85 hours per month are spent in the air, plus another 75-85 hours worked on the ground.

The Requirements

Person Specification

For the employment of cabin crew, airlines consider three key elements, these are: eligibility, suitability and specific requirements. Together, these three elements form a 'person specification'. This person specification is referred to throughout the selection process to determine each candidates suitability for the position.

Eligibility

Eligibility are the basic requirements which much be met in all circumstances. They are mostly based on facts and are likely to include:

- » Passport and/or visa requirements
- » Level of education
- » Previous experience
- » Language ability
- » Physical profile

Each airline's eligibility criteria will be different to some degree so, to avoid disappointment, it is advisable to investigate each airline's eligibility criteria before applying.

Suitability

Unlike eligibility, which is based on facts, suitability is based on 'Core Competencies' and are determined by observation. Core competencies are a collection of personal qualities, skills, knowledge and experience that are necessary for optimal performance in the job.

While there are several desirable characteristics for cabin crew, such as being confident, friendly and calm, there are four fundamental core competencies, these include:

- » Team spirit
- » Customer focus
- » Communication competence
- » Resilience

Specific Requirements

Following the eligibility and suitability requirements, airlines proceed to customise their requirements according to their specific standards and requirements.

These standards and requirements cover several criteria, and are subject to ongoing revision depending on the airlines present requirements. For example:

» Swimming ability
Some airlines have strict swimming requirements, which can range from a basic minimum distance, to more advanced abilities. Some airlines have no swimming requirements at all.

» Previous cabin crew experience
A new airline may view previous cabin crew experience as a prime requisite while a prestigious and well established airline may have no preference either way.

» Medical experience
If the airline determines that there is a shortage of crew with medical experience, this may be valued more highly.

» Language strength and range
If the airline extends its route network, a particular language fluency may become highly desirable

While performance is an obvious factor, the different and changing considerations which make up the person specification explain why it is possible to be rejected by one airline, but accepted by another, or unsuccessful on the first attempt, and then successful at the next.

Physical Profile

Due to the general physical nature of the job, airlines have stringent health and fitness guidelines in place for its cabin crew. While each airline will have its own requirements, the following guidelines will highlight the most common criteria.

Health & Fitness

As glamorous as the job appears, your health will be affected from the lack of routine, climatic and time zone changes, and long working hours so good health and strong immune system is essential for dealing with these conditions. In addition, you will need a good overall level of fitness for dealing with the general physical nature of the job, which includes opening and closing emergency doors and standing for long periods.

Important Note:

A comprehensive physical examination will be carried out at some stage, and whatever physical requirements have been set, you can be sure that these will be strictly enforced.

Incorrect measurements or unspecified conditions could result in your interview being terminated, or an offer of employment being withdrawn.

Officially, the Civil Aviation Authority (CAA) has outlined the following health guidelines for cabin crew:

» Free from any physical or mental illness which might lead to incapacitation or inability to perform cabin crew duties

» Normal cardio respiratory function

» Normal central nervous system

» Adequate visual acuity 6/9 with or without glasses

» Adequate hearing

» Normal function of ear, nose and throat

Height

Airlines have stringent minimum and maximum height restrictions. These height restrictions have been put in place because a very short person may have difficulties reaching the overhead compartments. Conversely, a very tall person may find the environment too cramped.

Height ranges vary from airline to airline, however, you can expect a typical minimum height of 5'2'' (158 cm) and a maximum of 6'2'' (188 cm).

Where an airline doesn't have a minimum height requirement, they may have a reach requirement instead. A reach requirement simply requires the ability to reach necessary components inside the aircraft which are typically between 6' (182 cm) and 6'10" (212 cm).

To determine candidates reach ability, a simple reach test may be conducted whereby a mark is placed on the wall, typically 6'10" from the floor, and the candidate is asked to reach for the line from their bare feet.

Weight

Airlines also have certain weight guidelines in place. These guidelines are based on 'Body Mass Index' (BMI) proportions and, as they are less restrictive, you shouldn't be too concerned if you slightly out of the range guidelines.

The Body Mass Index (BMI) is a formula used by health professionals to determine an adult's healthy body weight in relation to their height.

You can determine your own proportions, by referring to the BMI chart following...

Figure 1. Body Mass Index (BMI) Chart. Created by Vertex42.com and reproduced with permission

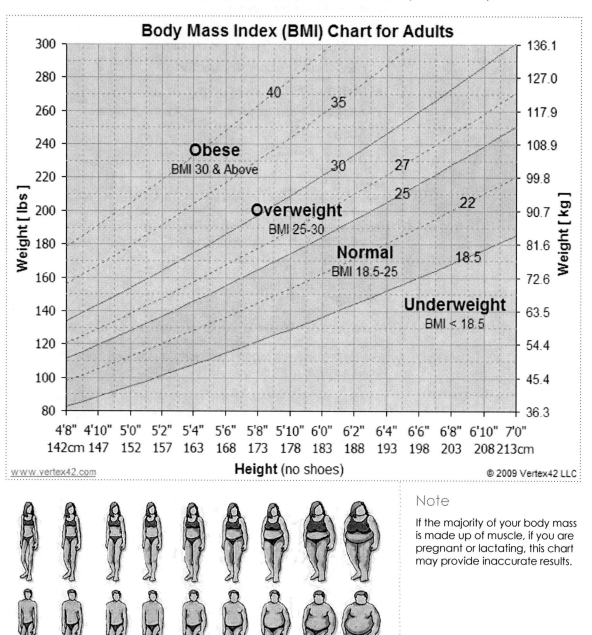

Note

If the majority of your body mass is made up of muscle, if you are pregnant or lactating, this chart may provide inaccurate results.

Figure 2. Visual (BMI) Chart. Created by Healthyweightforum.org

Age

Employment regulations generally prohibit discrimination on the grounds of age. It is, therefore, highly improbable that you will encounter an upper age limit beyond mandatory retirement age.

Lower age limits, however, do apply. While there is no set standard within the industry, it is typically between 18 and 21 years. Some airlines do recruit from aged 17, but these are exceptional cases.

Appearance

It is a mistaken belief that airlines only seek cabin crew who look like super-models. Appearance is important, but only to the extent of having a well groomed and presentable appearance.

A presentable appearance generally implies: no visible tattoos or facial piercings, and certainly no outrageous hair colours or styles.

The Airline

Airline Selection

Selecting potential airlines for which to apply is a fairly straightforward process and it is likely that you will have one or more airlines already in mind. However, selecting a potential employer is an important decision which should be considered carefully and not taken lightly.

Before you jump in, you need to consider the following:

The requirements
Do you meet the minimum requirements for the position? (See page 19)

Location
Cabin crew spend a certain amount of hours on standby duty and may be called in at short notice. As a result, crew are required to live within a certain radius, usually 60 minutes, of the base airport.

» If you live outside the maximum radius, would you be happy to relocate?

» If you fall within the maximum, would you be happy to travel this distance to and from every shift?

Similarly, if it is an international carrier, will you be happy to be away from your home and family for prolonged periods?

Salary & benefits
Are the salary and benefits sufficient to support your lifestyle?

Salaries for cabin crew vary greatly depending on the airline you are applying to, so you will need to check this yourself before you apply. You can expect to receive a set starting salary, plus an hourly flight pay and an overseas allowance.

Other benefits may include:

» Relocation

» Free or discounted accommodation

» Free duty transport

» Pay increments

» An annual ticket providing return travel to your home country (if the position involves relocation)

» Annual holiday leave entitlement

Note

Not all these benefits will be awarded and, as such, this list should be used as guidance only.

» Concessionary Air Travel privileges for yourself and members of your family (usually available after 6 months service)

» Annual cargo concessions

» Paid maternity and sick leave

» Medical & dental insurance and treatment

» Personal accident insurance worldwide for death or disablement.

» Personal effects insurance scheme whilst employees are travelling anywhere in the world on duty

» End-of-service benefits

» Utilities Allowance to assist in the payment of rent and utility bills

» Telephone Allowance to assist with phone rentals

Corporate culture

'Corporate Culture' is a term used to describe the collective ideas, attitudes, beliefs, behaviours and values that exist within an organisation. In essence, it is the character of the airline.

Careful consideration of the corporate culture should be awarded because if there is a mismatch, it is unlikely that you will be happy working within that airline in the long term.

Preliminary Research

Taking the time to research an airline you want to work for will enable you to ask intelligent questions, as well as answer any that are posed. Your informed knowledge will give a positive impression about you and your motivation to work for the airline, thus giving you a competitive edge over less informed candidates.

If you know nothing about the airline other than the colour of the uniform, the salary and their best destinations, you certainly won't create a positive impression.

There is no need to know the whole history of the airline, but you should at least know some basic information, such as:

» What is their route network?

» Are there any future plans for expansion or growth?

» Where is their base airport located?

» Who are the airline's major competitors?

» What do you like about this particular airline?

» How long have they been operating?

» Has the airline won any awards? If so, which ones?

Note:

Read through some of the airlines' literature. Their website is a great place to locate this kind of information.

Journal Notes

Journal Notes

Part 2

Prepare

....

Psychological Programming
Impression Management
Polish your Image
The Final Countdown

Psychological Programming

> **If you change the way you look at things, the things you look at change**
>
> Dr. Wayne Dyer

Our performance is dictated by our psychology. If our minds are preoccupied with doubt, we certainly won't perform well and are unlikely to be successful through each stage of the selection process.

Successful candidates share similar attitudes and beliefs, and have learned to manage their state. The good news is that these success patterns can be learned and duplicated. The following pages contain tips and techniques that will enable you to program your mind for success.

Manage your Mind Set

Limiting beliefs are erroneous assumptions we hold about our own capabilities. They lurk in our subconscious mind and lead to self-sabotaging behaviours which prevent us from achieving our desired goals. These beliefs are mostly acquired subconsciously through outside influences and, once accepted and imprinted into our subconscious mind, will dictate how well we perform, interact and grow.

To move forward, these limiting beliefs must be identified and challenged, and then replaced with empowering beliefs.

Identify
Clearly it would be impossible to challenge or change a belief that we are unaware of, so the first step to transformation involves identification.

Some limiting beliefs are obvious and can be easily identified by their all or nothing words, such as 'always' or 'never', or 'can't' or 'impossible'. For instance:

» My confidence always lets me down

» There's too much competition, I can't compete

» The interviews are impossible

» I never say the right thing

» I always fail

Some beliefs, however, are so deeply ingrained within our subconscious that we may not even be aware of their existence. To expose these, we can use a brainstorming session.

Brainstorming is a simple, yet powerful technique that produces raw material from the subconscious mind. To begin, simply sit down with a pad and pen and start writing down everything that comes to mind about the interview.

If you struggle for a place to begin, you could use the opening line "I want to pass the cabin crew interview but..." then proceed to fill in the page until you run out of buts.

Asking relevant questions may also help, for instance:

» What meanings could I have created based on my past disappointments?

» What pessimistic thoughts reoccur every time I think about the interview?

» What unnecessary assumptions do I make about the interview?

» How might my standards be affecting my ability to relax?

» Am I holding onto any stereotypical beliefs that are holding me back?

Challenge

Now that we have identified our limiting beliefs, the next step is to challenge them. By challenging our old beliefs, we create doubt. This doubt is all we need to be able to slot a new empowering belief in its place. Strong beliefs are not always easy to destroy. These can, however, be weakened when they are challenged.

» Challenge the beliefs directly
The first way to break down a limiting belief is to question its validity. Challenge yourself to find evidence against it, and build a case that proves the assumption wrong. You could ask yourself questions, such as: How do I know this? Is it impossible or just hard? Is there another way I could look at this? Could there be another truth here?

» Question the source
Do you know where your assumptions came from in the first place? Did you choose these beliefs or are they by-products of someone else's belief systems? Sometimes, realising a belief is not ours is enough to destroy it.

» Challenge their usefulness
During our life, we have picked up beliefs that have not served us or were only valid for a certain period, but we have held onto them ever since. Ask yourself: Does this belief still serve a useful purpose? Does it help me move closer to my goals? Does this belief help or hurt me? If this belief limits me, how can I quickly get rid of it?

Note:

To gain the most benefit from the technique, you should write continuously for several minutes without stopping or judging, and without regard for spelling or grammar. When finished, re-read what you have written and circle any limiting beliefs.

> It's not the events of our lives that shape us, but our beliefs as to what those events mean.
>
> Anthony Robbins

» Weigh the consequences
The avoidance of pain is a great motivator, so realising the negative consequences of our beliefs, may provide the motivation we need to destroy it. Ask yourself: What has this belief cost me in the past? If I don't change this belief now, what will the consequences be in the future?

Replace
In this final step, we will identify and install alternative empowering beliefs. To do this, we simply need to reinforce each new belief with sufficient evidence to support it. Ask yourself: What have I done in my past that could contribute as evidence? What activities and actions could I take now that would strengthen this belief?

Keep a journal and continue creating evidence towards it. The more ingrained you can make the belief, the more evidence it will begin to identify for itself, and the deeper rooted the belief will become.

This step isn't an overnight process. It does take time to imprint the belief deeply enough into your subconscious that it will stick long term and overpower the old limiting belief but, with repetition and reinforcement, positive changes will begin to happen in your life.

Use your Imagination

Since our brain knows no difference between real or imagined experiences, it is possible to use mental rehearsal and visualisation techniques to manipulate our physiology and improve our interview performance.

Find a quiet space where you're unlikely to be disturbed for 10-15 minutes and use these basic guidelines:

» Get into a comfortable position and allow your body to relax. Take a few deep breaths and, as you exhale, imagine all of the tension slowly leaving your body.

Disassociate

If you struggle to visualise the experience from your own associated perspective, try observing yourself from a disassociated onlooker's perspective first.

» Now imagine it is the day of your interview and begin to visualise the entire day, scene by scene, in your subconscious. When running through the events in your mind, imagine feeling relaxed, yet energised as you converse effortlessly with other candidates and the recruiters. Observe how others warm to your friendly and confident nature. Imagine your composure as you intelligently answer the interviewer's questions.

» Make each scene as vivid and real as you can. Bring it closer, make the colours richer, sense the atmosphere in the room, and introduce sounds and feelings. Really intensify the experience.

» When you are pleased with the imagined performance, begin to introduce challenging scenarios for different characters you may encounter, questions you may be asked, and pressure you may be put under.

Using this rehearsal technique for just twenty minutes a day will train your brain to actually perform the new skills and behaviours.

Repetition is the key to success with this technique. The more you practice, the better you will get and the more confident you will feel.

Anchor your State

Anchoring is an NLP (Neuro Linguistic Programming) term which describes a process whereby certain psychological states, positive or negative, become associated with and can be triggered by a certain stimulus.

Using certain techniques, it is possible to anchor positive states so that we can readily access them on demand, or we can break the association of undesirable states using collapsing techniques.

Create an anchor

» Step 1: Identify
To begin the process of creating an anchor, we first need to identify the desirable state. For instance: confidence, calmness, assertiveness.

» Step 2: Locate a memory
Next we need to recall a particular time in our life when we have felt the desired state. The context is unimportant, but the experience must have been a powerful one.

» Step 3: Get into state
With an experience in mind, mentally put yourself back into that experience. Use all your senses to make the experience as vivid and intense as you can. What did you see? What could you hear? Where there any smells present? How did you look? How did you feel? Now really focus in and intensify those feelings.

» Step 4: Anchor the state
When the desired state has been captured and the feeling is about to hit its peak, it is time to anchor those feelings. This is done by firing off a unique combination of cues.

The cue combination can include one which is visual, one auditory, and one kinaesthetic. For example, pinching the skin above your knuckles, while visualising the colour blue, and saying the word 'YES' is a unique cue combination that would be appropriate.

Timing

The timing of your cues is critical. To be most effective, only fire up your cues at the very peak moment of the state, when it is most intense.

Uniqueness

The kinaesthetic cue you select should be unique. For example, scratching your palm, pinching the flesh above your knuckles and pulling the lobe of your ear are all unique gestures.

Repetition

Repetition really makes all the difference with this technique. The more you rehearse, the stronger you anchors will be.

» Step 5: Repeat
To really condition the anchor, repeat this procedure at least five times. The more repetitions, the stronger the anchor will be.

» Step 6: Test
Now that our anchor has been installed, we need to test its effectiveness. To do this, we simply need to fire off our unique cue combination that we set up in step 4.

For best results, break state for a few moments and think of something completely unrelated.

If the anchor has been a success, the desired state should be experienced within 10-15 seconds. If the feeling is not satisfactory, further reinforcement repetitions may be carried out, or the power of anchor stacking may be introduced.

Collapse an anchor

» Step 1: Identify
Before we begin the process of collapsing an anchor, we first need to identify the problem state (e.g. panic, anger, anxiety) and decide an alternative desired state that we would like to create in its place (e.g. confidence, calmness, assertiveness).

» Step 2 : Create
Next, we begin the process of creating anchors (See above). First we will create an anchor for the desirable state we want to capture. Then, we need to repeat the process for the undesirable state we want to collapse.

Quick & Dirty Tip

To add bulk to a positive anchor, play videos that put you in positive states and fire your positive anchors during the peak state moments.

Important

The positive anchor must be stronger than the problem anchor. If the reverse is true, further reinforcement should be carried out to strengthen the positive anchor.

In creating these two anchors, we want to create the desirable anchor according to the steps outlined previously, however, the undesirable state should be created with less intensity in order to give the positive state more power.

This can be done effectively by simply visualising the negative state in less context, using fewer senses, and only using one kinaesthetic cue (be sure this cue is different to the one selected for the positive anchor)

Stacking Anchors

The process of stacking anchors adds significant strength to anchors and simply involves eliciting several positive states into one set of cues.

» Step 3: Repeat
To really condition the anchors, repeat the procedure at least five times. The more repetitions, the stronger the anchor will be.

» Step 4: Test
Now that our anchors have been installed, we need to test their effectiveness. To do this, we simply need to fire off our unique cue combination.

For best results, break state for a few moments and think of something completely unrelated.

If the anchor has been a success, the state should be experienced within 10-15 seconds. If the feeling is not satisfactory, further reinforcement repetitions may be carried out, or the power of anchor stacking may be introduced.

» Step 5: Collapse
Finally, we begin the process of collapsing our problem anchor.

To do this, we simply fire both anchors at the same time. As you do this, your physiology will feel somewhat confused as it tries to achieve both states simultaneously. If the positive anchor has been created strong enough, the negative anchor will begin to clear. At this stage, we can let the negative anchor release, while we continue to fire and hold onto the positive state.

» Step 6: Test
To test the success of the collapse, break state for a few moments and try to re-fire the negative anchor. The result should be neutral. If the state persists the procedure may be repeated, using the power of stacking positive anchors.

Ask Resourceful Questions

When we ask questions of ourselves, we prompt our minds to search our internal memory archive for reasons and/or evidence to support those questions. So, whether we ask an empowering question, such as: "How can I achieve this?' or "Why am I so lucky?" or a disempowering question, such as: "Why does this always happen to me?" or "Why can't I ever get this right?" our brains will work to bring forth answers.

Wouldn't you rather have your brain bring back answers that create happiness and success? Well, why don't you make yourself a commitment to only ask empowering questions of yourself from this point forward? It's simple to do, and will really enhance the quality of your life.

Replace:

» "What's the point? I never pass anyway"

» "I always get nervous in interviews"

» "Why can't I be confident?"

With:

» "What steps can I take that will increase my chances of success?"

» "What can I do to manage my emotions?"

» "How can I feel confident right now?"

Re Frame your Words

Our confidence is shaped by our words. Changing the words we use can instantly change the way we think, feel and act.

For example, if we view the interview as a challenge and opportunity to grow, rather than a difficulty, our failures as feedback, and our mistakes as learning experiences, our whole physiology will become much more positive.

Similarly, when we say 'I can't', we are setting limitations on ourselves and will instantly cut ourself off from all possibility. Rather, we should try asking, 'how can I?' as this will challenge our brain to come up with solutions.

> I have not failed.
> I've just found 10,000
> ways that won't work

Thomas Edison

Adjust your Physiology

Our physiology has a direct impact on our psyche. Therefore, if we make some simple adjustments to our physiology, we can easily adjust our mood. To illustrate this point more clearly, try the following experiments:

Imagine for a moment that you harbour some self esteem issues and have a serious lack of confidence. Now ask yourself the following questions and then perform the appropriate corresponding movements:

If I were confident...

» How would I move?

» How would I sit?

» How would I sound?

» How would I look?

» How would I breathe?

» What gestures would I make?

Did you notice the change? Now try this:

» Curl your facial muscles up into a smile. Now, while maintaining this beautiful smile, try to become depressed or angry.

Now, anytime in the future that you find yourself in a negative state, use this technique to deliberately change it. If you feel unconfident, increase your confidence by acting like someone who has an abundance of it. If you feel sad, act like someone that is happy. If you feel tired, become energetic. If you feel angry... and so on.

Appear Confident

» Stand/sit tall with your shoulders back and head high
» Present a warm, relaxed smile
» Use open gestures
» Hold eye contact
» Breathe slowly and deeply
» Move with energy

Submodalities

Submodalities represent our five senses. I.e. Visual, auditory, kinaesthetic, olfactory and gustatory.

Make the Swish

The swish pattern is a simple, yet very powerful sub modality technique which enables us to address unwanted and damaging behaviour responses, and replace them with appropriate and empowering ones. In essence, this method reprograms our brains neuro-associations.

For illustrative purposes, let's imagine that in stress provoking situations, such as an interview, we feel compelled to bite our nails. Clearly, this is an unwanted and unhelpful habit which does not create a positive impression. Using the swish method, we can completely and immediately eliminate this bad habit. Here's how we use the swish pattern:

» Step 1: Identify the problem behaviour
First, we need to identify the problem behaviour. This could be one of many common problems such as: Stammering, blushing or trembling. Now, create an image that represents the habit or behaviour.

» Step 2: Identify the desired behaviour
Now identify an alternative behaviour and create a corresponding mental image of this state. For example: In the case of stammering, you may see yourself conversing clearly and effortlessly.

» Step 3: Identify suitable sub modalities
Identify and apply a sub modality that will reduce the desire for the problem behaviour in step 1 (E.g. Use a monochrome, unfocused image) and another that will increase desire for the empowering behaviour in step 2 (E.g. Increase the size, sounds and brightness).

» Step 4: Time to swish
Finally, we will use the swish pattern to replace the problem state. To do this, we will take the problem image from step 1, with the sub modality applied, and place it prominently in our mind.

Next we will take the desired image, also with the sub modality applied, and imagine it being placed into a sling shot. Now, imagine the sling shot drawing the image far into the distance, feel the tension of the elastic. Then, when ready to activate the swish, simply release the image from the sling shot and allow it to come hurtling forwards so that it smashes through the original image.

Allow the image to grow bigger, brighter, and more colourful. Let it completely fill your mind to make it really compelling.

To create even more power, we can include auditory and kinaesthetic cues to the pattern. For instance: we could say "whoosh" or "swish" while throwing a fist into the air.

» Step 5: Repeat
To reinforce the new behaviour, repeat step 4 at least 10 times in quick succession, each time making it faster. To avoid looping and reversing the pattern, it is important to break state between each cycle so that we always begin from and break through the starting image.

> Repetition of the same thought or physical action develops into a habit which, repeated frequently enough, becomes an automatic reflex
>
> Norman Vincent Peale

Find your Focus

What we focus on has a direct impact on how we feel and what we experience. So, when we focus on what we don't want, such as 'not feeling stressed' and 'not feeling unconfident' we only serve to attract more of these feelings because we are focusing all of our attention on them. Rather, we should focus on what we do want.

For instance:

Instead of:	Focus on:
Don't feel stressed	Feel calm and relaxed
Don't feel anxious	Feel alert and confident
Don't be upset	Feel joyful

Create Compelling Reasons

There may be challenging periods that arise during your interview which cause you to question your motives. If you have compelling reasons for wanting the job, your conviction will give you the driving force you need to carry you through these challenging moments.

So, ask yourself:

- » Why do I really want this job?
- » How will this job change my life?
- » How will I feel when I am successful?
- » What would I enjoy about the job?

Affirm & Incant

Affirmations and incantations are used to promote positive changes in our life.

Affirmations are short positive statements which are repeated several times in order to impress on our subconscious mind. To perform an affirmation, we simply take our chosen statement, for example "I am confident and successful in everything I do", and repeat it several times in quick succession with all the conviction and passion we can muster.

An incantation is a supercharged affirmation which also engages our physiology. This action of getting our body involved creates a much more powerful outcome.

> You become what you think about
>
> Earl Nightingale

Depending on how deeply ingrained our beliefs are, we may experience some strong resistance as our brain attempts to challenge the positive messages it is receiving. Thus, the effectiveness of both techniques relies on repetition, conviction and passion. The stronger your concentration, the deeper your faith and the more feeling you inject, the stronger the results will be and the faster changes will begin to occur.

The process of creating an affirmation involves a simple two step process:

» Step 1:
Think about areas in your life which you would like to improve and write them down. When you do this, focus on what you do want rather than what you don't want.

For example: I want to be confident
                    I want to be more assertive
                    I want to be liked
                    I want be calm

» Step 2:
Go through your list and write a positive affirmation   for   every desire. These may be in the present tense, such as: "I feel calm, confident and in control", or they may be releasing in nature, such as: "Every day I feeling calmer, more confident and in control". Your choice will depend on strength of resistance you experience. If there is only a slight feeling of resistance, continue with the present tense. If, however, the resistance is strong, you may start with a softer releasing statement until you begin to break through the barrier.

Sample present tense affirmations:

» "I experience love and joy with every part of my body"

» "I feel calm and am self disciplined"

» "I am a unique and special persona"

» "I am beautiful because I am me"

» "I am respected and admired by others"

Sample releasing affirmations:

» "I am feeling happier and more self confident"

» "Every day I am feeling calmer and more disciplined"

» "I can feel my confidence growing stronger and stronger"

» "I love and appreciate myself more every day"

Supercharge

To supercharge your incantations further, try singing or chanting them.

Common Concerns

Unless there is some form of medical condition present, each of the common concerns listed below are generally symptoms of an underlying psychological element, such as anxiety. If these symptoms are psychologically driven, using the techniques described within this session will help manage, and even eliminate, these symptoms. However, there are specific techniques that can be used to minimise their impact.

Challenge: Anxiety

Nervous feelings before an interview are quite legitimate and most people can relate to feeling tense or fearful on the run up to such an event. In fact, a little interview anxiety can make us more alert and really enhance our performance, so we would never want to completely eliminate interview anxiety. However, when that anxiety becomes strong enough to negatively affect our clarity of thought and dialogue, some anxiety management techniques should be introduced.

» Proper preparation
Anxiety can be the result of poor preparation. If you anticipate potential questions, prepare appropriate answers, research the airline and understand the requirements of the job, you will be better mentally prepared. If your mind is prepared, it makes sense that you will feel calmer, and more confident in yourself and your ability to handle the interview.

» Deep breathing
Deep breathing will steady your rapid heartbeat, strengthen your shallow breathing, provide your brain with vital oxygen and make you more alert.

Technique: Find a comfortable seating or standing position. Now, over the count of seven, inhale slowly and deeply through your nose. You should notice your stomach expand as your lungs begin to fill with oxygen.

Now, over the count of 10-13 seconds, begin to exhale slowly through your mouth, allowing your stomach to gradually flatten. As you release the oxygen from your lungs allow your shoulders to relax and feel the tension release.

Continue this pattern of in and out breaths until your breathing becomes steady and the anxiety subsides.

» Remediation
Hypnotherapy, Cognitive Behavioural Therapy (CBT) and Neuro Linguistic Programming (NLP) sessions are very effective at dealing with deep rooted anxiety issues.

Recommended:

For those of you interested in learning more about this kind of intervention, I highly recommend a program by *Anthony Robbins* called 'Personal Power II'.

Further information about this program can be found at www.tonyrobbins.com

» Medication
If you find your anxiety levels quite literally overwhelm you at interviews, you may be considering medication. While this is a method I don't advocate, there are over the counter supplements, such as Kalms, St John's Wort, and Bachs Rescue Remedy, which can really help take the edge off anxiety. Otherwise, stronger prescription medications such as Xanex or Beta Blockers may be prescribed by your medical practitioner.

Challenge: Sweating

» Dress Colours
Black, navy and pure white will help disguise sweat marks, as will the camouflaging nature of patterns. Avoid: Light colours such as pale blue or grey.

» Dress Fabrics
Wear breathable fabrics such as: 100% cotton, pima cotton, seersucker, linen, 100% wool, merino, and cashmere. Avoid: Corduroy, flannel, silk, polyester and polyester blends, nylon, and acetate

» Dress Style
Wear loose fitting over and under garments for maximum air flow. Add layers, such as a suit jacket, waistcoat or cardigan, to disguise sweating.

» Antiperspirant
Use a clear, unperfumed antiperspirant. Beware: Antiperspirant can leave a film residue on your clothing. To avoid these stains, allow the antiperspirant to dry completely before putting on your shirt.

» Keep fresh
During bathroom breaks, wash your hands with lukewarm water. Blot your hands dry with a tissue and finish off with a light mist of a clear antiperspirant. Avoid: Cold or hot water, air dryers and sticky antiperspirants.

» Seek medical advice
Individuals with Hyperhidrosis, may seek the advice of a medical professional or dermatologist. Both can advise and prescribe suitable treatments, such as: Prescription strength antiperspirants and Botox.

Challenge: Not Enough Eye Contact
Good eye contact is one of the most important factors of body language. Shifty eyes, or complete avoidance of contact can suggest dishonesty, rudeness or lack of confidence. If you find eye contact anxiety provoking and uncomfortable, the following techniques will certainly help.

Warning

Always talk with your doctor before taking a medicine for the first time.

Challenge: Cotton mouth

» Keep fully hydrated by drinking plenty of water on the run up to the event. Fill up on water during breaks and periodically sip on water throughout the assessment.

» Stimulate saliva flow by adding a splash of lemon juice to your water bottle, sucking on sugar free candy or chewing sugarless gum. Gently biting your tongue can also activate the glands that stimulate saliva flow.

» Avoid salty and sugary foods, alcohol (including alcohol based mouthwash), caffeinated beverages and tobacco products as these inhibit saliva flow and dry the mouth out.

Note:

You should aim to maintain eye contact 80 percent to 90 percent of the time.

» Use a mirror
Practice your eye contact by using your own mirrored image as a guinea pig. When you see yourself in the mirror every day, make a point of looking directly into your own eyes.

» Fake it
Rather than look directly into the eyes, you can fake it by either directing your gaze at their eyebrows, forehead, or bridge of the nose. This is not a permanent solution by any means, but it will certainly ease you into the process.

» Avoid staring
In an attempt to forge eye contact, we may begin to stare. This can indicate aggression and make others feel uncomfortable. To avoid this extreme, lighten your gaze and keep it friendly. This can be achieved by allowing your eyes to go slightly out of focus.

» Use opportunities
If you have notes, you can temporarily break eye contact as you refer to these. Also, f there is a second recruitment officer present, this will give you another opportunity to break eye contact as you periodically direct your focus back and forth between the two.

Challenge: Blanking out
Even with all the preparation in the world, our mind can betray us and draw a blank at the most inopportune moment. If this happens, take a deep breath, remain composed and employ some of the following techniques:

» Refer to your résumé
Your résumé provides an immediate memory jog in these instances, so refer to it as and when necessary. You may also want to jot down some key words or phrases inside a professional looking notebook beforehand.

» Wait a moment
You don't have to always answer questions immediately. It is perfectly permissible to pause and collect your thoughts before proceeding with a response. In fact, taking the time to think through your response can make you appear deliberate and thoughtful. Answering without regard for your answer can make you look impulsive.

» Be honest
If you don't have relative experience in a particular area, or simply don't know the answer, you need to be honest and say so. At this point, you could offer an alternative piece of information.

» Stall
If you feel you can get away with it, reflect the question back to allow yourself a little more thinking time.

» Stay composed
Some recruiters will purposely throw in some curve ball questions to see how you react to pressure and think on your feet. In these cases, the interviewer is probably more interested in observing your reaction than they are about the answer you provide. So, stay calm and do your best to answer in a confident manner. In the worst case, simply be honest and admit you don't know the answer.

Challenge: Involuntary facial motions
Unless there is a medical condition present, involuntary facial twitching and trembling are generally ensuing of overly stressed muscles, such as forced smiling. These distressing symptoms are especially pronounced during an interview when we feel compelled to smile, or are attempting to conceal our nerves. To gain relief from these symptoms, we simply need to control how and when we smile.

Maintaining a constant grin is not only unnecessary and uncomfortable, it will also look insincere. Gentle and understated smiles are more than appropriate for prolonged periods, and full toothed smiles should be reserved for introductions and the occasional injection during conversation.

Next time you feel your facial muscles begin to tense, try relaxing your smile and see what a difference it makes.

Challenge: Fidgeting
Fidgeting, tapping and excessive gesturing with give the appearance of uncertainty, nervousness and unpreparedness. To effectively manage these movements, use the techniques outlined below.

» Identify
If you are unsure of any habits you may have, ask a friend, partner or coworker for their views. Alternatively, record yourself in a short mock interview and examine the footage. Mark down any ineffective mannerisms you can identify (playing with your pen, drumming your fingers, touching your face or hair, clearing your throat, or rubbing your nose) and then begin the process of eliminating each of them.

» Beware of props
Props can easily exaggerate any fidgeting, so if you have a pen, résumé or bag with you, avoid fiddling with them. Be equally mindful of jewellery, such as twirling earrings or a finger ring.

» Mind your hands
If the movements you employ are subtle, it is perfectly okay to gesture your arms and hands to endorse your words. Subtle means, keeping the movements below shoulder height and above the waist. If you find your movements become excessive or distracting, simply intertwine your fingers and rest your hands on the table or clasped loosely in your lap.

Challenge: Blushing

» Go green
A purposeful green pigmented concealer or foundation will minimise the impact of redness.

» Seek medical advice
Blushing which is caused by a medical condition should be treated by a medical professional. Prescription medication may be prescribed.

Challenge: Vocal paralysis

Under severe pressure, our voice may become partially paralysed. The physical symptoms of this may include stuttering, a weak and shaky vocal tone, or an unusually high pitch. These symptoms can be managed by adopting the following techniques:

» Speak in shorter phrases
» Slow your pace
» Control your breathing by using steady in-out breaths
» Maintain an upright posture
» Ignore the symptoms until they naturally relieve themselves
» Seek the assistance of a vocal coach

Gestures

Further information about gesturing and their usage can be found on page 49

Challenge: Perceived Arrogance

Sometimes, a high level of confidence may be misconstrued as arrogance. If you feel you are sometimes wrongly labelled as arrogant, the following guidelines will help you maintain your confidence, while avoiding this assumption.

» Be open
  We all have weaknesses, to say otherwise will certainly make you appear arrogant. Be clear about what you do and don't know, and be prepared to listen and learn from others.

» Be humble
  Act with humility when you are recognised for a job well done. Acknowledge the effort of others by sharing and giving praise where appropriate, and be accountable when errors transpire.

» Be approachable
  To make yourself appear more approachable, use open and inviting body language, and adopt a warm, friendly expression. Inject some personality into your conversations, make good use of eye contact (see above) and remember to use peoples names.

» Be considerate
  Genuinely acknowledge and compliment the hard work and efforts of others. Listen to and respect others opinions, and avoid interrupting when others are speaking.

Three Steps to Mastery

There are three basic steps to mastering the techniques introduced within this session, these are:

» Repeat
  When we learn any new skill, we need to practice the skill many times until we can do it automatically. Studies suggest seven to twelve repetitions.

» Apply
  When we are comfortable with our grasp of the new skill, we need to apply it to our daily life.

» Reinforce
  When we have mastered the new skill, we need to keep it strong with continual use.

Put a little time and effort into mastering these techniques, and you will master any area of your life, even beyond the interview.

Use it or lose it
Jimmy Connors

Journal Notes

Impression Management

Invent your Introduction

First impressions are absolutely critical for interview success. The impression you provide within the first few minutes will be the one that sticks and, anything following, will become merely a confirmation of that first impression. So, to assist you in getting off to the very best start, I have devised some tips that will make you appear confident, friendly, relaxed and professional.

On arrival

Upon arriving at the venue, approach the reception desk and introduce yourself, your purpose and whom you are expecting to meet. For example:

> "Hello. My name is Jane Doe and I'm here for an interview with Carrie Loren"

Once signed in, thank the receptionist and take a seat in the waiting area.

Warning

Take great care with candidate introductions, and read their body language on approach. Some candidates may be stand-offish because they see you as competition, while others may need some alone time with their thoughts. If you feel any sense of displeasure from your approach, back off immediately.

Meeting the candidates

If you are attending an open day or group selection process where other candidates will be present, you will have many introductions to contend with. These introductions are just as important as any other and must not be underestimated.

Candidate introductions should be handled in much the same way as any other, however, you may keep these slightly less formal if you wish. As you approach the candidate(s), smile and make eye contact, then say hello and introduce yourself. In a one to one introduction, offer a handshake if you so desire. In a group introduction, a handshake is unnecessary. If the candidate(s) responds positively to your approach, you may engage in further small talk.

Meeting the recruiter(s)

When you meet each recruiter for the first time, be sure to stand up straight, make eye contact and smile. Then, allow the recruiter to initiate the introduction and the handshake.

» If they greet you by name, your response should be:
"Hello Ms. Loren. It's a pleasure to meet you".

» If an introduction is needed, simply say:
"I'm Jane Doe. It's a pleasure to meet you" or
"Hello Ms. Loren. Pleased to meet you. I'm Jane Doe"

At this stage, pleasantries may be initiated by the recruiter as a way to break the ice. Just follow their lead and go with the flow.

Consider your Communication

Because effective communication skills are essential for interview success, it is important to be mindful of how our communication is received. This means that we must consider not only the words we use, but also how our tonality and body language complement or contradict those words.

Consider the following communication guidelines:

Word Choice

Words are important because they communicate and convey our message succinctly. So, even at a low 7% accountability, our word choice can mean the difference between a powerful, captivating and influential exchange, and a weak, disempowering and ineffective one. To create the desired response, consider the following guidelines:

» Action Words
Action words are positive, powerful and directive, and should be used abundantly. Action words include: Communicated, conveyed, directed, listened, persuaded, arranged, handled and improved. *A complete list of action verbs can be found on page 101*

» Filler Words
Anyways, you know how when you are, like, really nervous, and you ,ummm, find it hard to verbalise and stuff, and you say silly things that, kind of, make you sound, like, kind of, unprofessional and maybe, like, inarticulate?

The useless and annoying verbal mannerisms used in the above example "you know," "like," "in other words," "kind of," "ummm," and "anyways." should be avoided at all costs. Besides sounding unprofessional, they also distract attention from the message.

» Undermining Words
Words and phrases such as 'I think,' 'I hope,' 'maybe,' 'sort of,' 'perhaps,' 'I guess,' all undermine your message and credibility by creating the impression that you don't trust your own knowledge or opinion. Eliminating these phrases will drastically improve the quality of any message.

» Jargon, Slang and Clichés
Specialist terminology and informal expressions can confuse an outside audience. Avoid these where possible, and stick to simple, clear and coherent language.

7% Words
38% Tonality
55% Body Language

The 1971 study, conducted by Albert Mehrabian, suggests that our words account for only 7% of our overall communication, while tonality accounts for a further 38% and body language accounts for a massive 55%.

Tonality

Our tonality plays a key role in sending the correct messages. So, if our aim is to project confidence, enthusiasm and expertise, it is important to exercise control and awareness of our tonality throughout our interactions.

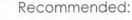

» Pitch
Pitch refers to the degree of highness and lowness in our voice. A variation in our pitch creates meaning, adds clarity and makes what we are saying more interesting. For instance: A rise in our pitch suggests we are asking a question, which indicates doubt, uncertainty and hesitation. A fall in pitch indicates a statement, which further suggests certainty and assurance.

» Tempo
Tempo refers to the speed of our voice. If we speak too slowly, we risk losing the interest and attention of our audience. If we speak too fast, others may find us difficult to follow. The key is to maintain a pace which is fast enough to maintain interest, yet slow enough to be clear.

» Volume
Volume refers to the loudness of our voice. Speaking in a loud volume suggests aggression, while a quiet volume indicates shyness and makes it difficult to be heard. The key to determining the appropriate volume is to keep your voice loud enough to be heard, but soft enough to be clear. Modulation of volume can also be introduced to keep the speech interesting and add extra emphasis.

» Articulation
Articulation refers to our vocal clarity. Regardless of our pitch, tempo, volume and accent, we need to make a conscious effort to enunciate clearly.

Body Language

The way we carry ourselves, the gestures we use and our facial expressions communicate all sorts of messages, so learning to control certain aspects of these can help us to convey the message of a well-balanced, confident individual.

» Gestures
We use open gestures when we are feeling confident and relaxed, and are being honest and sincere. Therefore, to be perceived as relaxed, sincere and confident, keep your arms unfolded, your legs uncrossed and your palms open.

Recommended:

For those of you interested in voice training, I highly recommend a program by *Roger Love* called 'The Perfect Voice'.

Further information about this program can be found at www.rogerlove.com

Caution

Because gestures are culture specific, it is important to exercise caution when around people from other cultures.

Different meanings may be unintentionally conveyed, and can easily lead to confusion and misunderstanding.

Gesturing can also be useful for adding emphasis to what we are saying and, if the movements we employ are subtle and controlled, it is perfectly okay to use gestures to express ourselves and endorse our words. For best results, keep any movements below shoulder level, but above the waistline.

If you find your movements become excessive or distracting, simply rest your hands on the table or loosely in your lap.

Open Palms
Open palms signify honesty and give the impression of a relaxed and confident person.

Steepling fingers
This gesture is understood to be a sign of confidence and authority.

Nodding your head in agreement when the recruiter is speaking will signal that you are listening and understand. However, be careful not to over emphasise the movement.

» Movement
The way we carry ourselves is a powerful indicator of how we feel. To be perceived as confident and professional, walk briskly with an erect posture. Keep your shoulders back, your arms loosely at your side, and chin parallel to the floor.

» Posture
To portray the image of a confident and motivated person, adopt an upright and attentive posture that is open, yet relaxed. Keep your chin parallel to the floor, shoulders back and spine straight.

If seated, lean slightly forward with your hands loosely in your lap, or on the table. Place both feet flat on the floor, or cross your ankles.

If standing, keep your arms loosely at your side or behind your back and plant your feet about 8-10 inches apart. If standing for long periods, place one foot slightly in front of the other to allow you to smoothly and unnoticeably shift weight between your feet.

Top Ten Negative Gestures

» Finger Pointing
» Fist Pounding
» Karate Chopping
» Finger Drumming
» Hand Wringing
» Oversized Gestures
» Feet Tapping
» Arm Crossing
» Pen Clicking
» Hair Twirling

Tip
To achieve good posture, stand with your back to the wall and look straight ahead. In this position, your head, shoulders and bottom should touch the wall.

Avoid

» The John Wayne:
Feet wide apart with hands on hips.
» The fig leaf:
Feet close together with hands crossed over genital area.

Both stances will guarantee you a loss of respect and power instantly.

» Facial Expressions
Our facial expressions convey a wide range of attitudes, feelings and emotions, and these can have a significant impact on our ability to connect with others. Because of this, it is important to be aware of the story our face is telling and work to convey an attentive, sincere and interested expression.

A positive expression can certainly include a smile, but doesn't necessarily imply its inclusion. In fact, maintaining a constant smile is not only uncomfortable, it is also completely unnecessary. Instead, an open expression that includes a gentle and understated smile, soft eyes and slightly elevated eyebrows will result in a soft and pleasant expression.

Large smiles should be reserved for introductions and the occasional injection during conversation.

» Handshake
Your hand shake says a lot about you. A firm handshake conveys confidence, assertiveness and professionalism. A weak, limp handshake suggests shyness and insecurity, and a strong, crushing handshake indicates aggression and dominance.

To perform a professional and confident handshake, follow these simple guidelines:

Before connecting for the handshake establish eye contact, smile and lean slightly forward. As you extend your right hand, keep your hand straight and thumb pointing upwards. When your hands connect engage a firm, but not crushing, grip. Shake one to three times, for a duration of 1-3 seconds, and break away.

» Eye Contact
Good eye contact is one of the most important factors of body language. Shifty eyes, or complete avoidance of contact can suggest dishonesty, boredom, rudeness, insecurity or shyness.

If you find eye contact anxiety provoking and uncomfortable, direct your gaze at their eyebrows, forehead, or bridge of the nose. This is not a permanent solution by any means, but it will certainly ease you into the process.

In an attempt to forge eye contact, be aware not to stare as this can indicate aggression and make others feel uncomfortable. To avoid this extreme, lighten your gaze and keep it friendly. This can be achieved by allowing your eyes to go slightly out of focus.

If you have notes, you can temporarily break eye contact as you refer to these. Also, f there is a second recruitment officer present, this will give you another opportunity to break eye contact as you periodically direct your focus back and forth between the two.

» Eye Cues

As with our facial expressions, our eyes reveal much about how we are feeling. This could be through our eye contact, blink rate, or eye movements.

We blink, on average, 10 times per minute. When we are relaxed, our blink rate reflects this slower rate. When we are anxious, uncomfortable or being dishonest, our blink rate increases.

Our eye movements, eye accessing cues, reveal whether we are accessing a memory, or constructing one. While it is debated as to whether we can catch someone lying by watching their eye direction, we can certainly determine what sensory system they are accessing.

VC - Visual Constructed

This would be the direction a persons eyes moved in when they are constructing new visual images.

AC - Auditory Constructed

This would be the direction a persons eyes moved in when they 'auditorily construct' a sound in their mind.

Eye Accessing Cues
Based on a right handed person while facing them.

VC
Visual Constructed

VR
Visual Remembered

AC
Auditory Constructed

AR
Auditory Remembered

K
Kinaesthetic

AD
Auditory Digital

AR - Auditory Remembered

This would be the direction a persons eyes moved in when they are remembering sounds from the past.

AD - Auditory Digital

This would be the direction a persons eyes moved in when they access internal dialogue

K - Kinaesthetic

This would be the direction a persons eyes move in as they recall a smell, feeling or taste.

VR - Visual Remembered

This would be the direction a persons eyes moved in when they are visually remembering the past.

Communication Barriers

Barriers to effective communication may arise for a number of reasons. When these barriers do occur, we are forced to become even more effective in our ability to communicate. The strategies below will help overcome some of these more effectively.

» Language
Language barriers are a common challenge in interview settings. If you struggle with the native language of the airline, or have a very strong accent, speak slowly and clearly, ask for clarification and check for understanding, avoid idioms and jargon, use gestures and be specific, listen actively and be patient.

» Cultural
Because every culture has its own set of values, beliefs and behaviours, the potential for confusion and misunderstanding is high. Even when we speak the same language, these differences can lead to challenges. To effectively connect with an individual from a culturally different background, it is important to be sensitive and respectful, avoid prejudice and stereotyping, and be aware of using questionable language and gestures.

» Gender
Barriers in communication between genders exist primarily because men and women have different communication patterns. To overcome these barriers, it is important to appreciate, learn and understand the different strengths and styles that exist.

While men tend to be more direct and factual, women tend to be indirect and tactful. Men have a preference for reason and logic, are competitive and are interested in power, rank and status. Women are empathetic and feeling oriented. They value relationships and like to build rapport. Men communicate to exchange information and solve problems, while women communicate to share and a build connection.

» Emotional
Emotional barriers within an interview situation manifest themselves through fear, shyness or restraint. When we feel distracted by these emotional states, our ability to communicate at an effective level is severely inhibited. We may wrongly interpret the actions and words of others, and may not effectively express our own opinion. We may even stop listening to the other person as our internal dialogue takes over.

To effectively deal with these barriers, it is important to treat the underlying cause of such emotions. This can be achieved with psychological intervention (see pages 31-39).

Create a Connection

To form a memorable impression and influence the recruiters hiring decision in our favour, it is important to make an effort to connect. Mirroring is a very effective connecting strategy because of its ability to create rapport and trust.

As the name suggests, mirroring is a process whereby our communication style and body language mirror those of the recruiter. Providing our imitations are subtle and not obvious in any way, adapting our speaking style and movements can help the recruiter relate with us and feel more comfortable.

Communication Style

Mirroring communication style can be done through using similar words or phrases, matching the sensory style, or mimicking the pitch, tempo and volume of their voice.

» Words and Phrases
   We can make a fantastic psychological impact simply by injecting the recruiters own terminology and sequence of words into our answers. For example, if the interviewer points out that they are looking for and value a candidate who is 'team spirited, customer focused and efficient', simply stating that we are 'good with customers, work well in a team and always make an effort', while implying the same values, will not create the same strong psychological impact.

» Pitch, Tempo and Volume
   Matching our pitch, tempo and volume to the recruiters speaking style will make us appear in tune to what they are saying. This will speed up the rapport process and greatly improve our chances of creating a favourable impression.

» Sensory Style
   While we all use a mix of the sensory styles: Visual, kinaesthetic and auditory, we tend to have a dominant style that we gravitate towards. If, during the course of the interview, it becomes obvious that the recruiter has a preference towards a particular sensory style, you can adjust your style accordingly to establish a deeper connection.

   Visual people prefer to see how things are done rather than just talk about them. They are neat and orderly and take pride in their appearance. They speak rather quickly and use words that reflect their visual style, such as: 'I see what you mean', 'It looks to me like...', 'I imagine that...'

Auditory people like to use their voice and can easily go into lengthy discussions. They enjoy reading aloud and will often talk to themselves while working. Their style can be identified by their medium pace of speech and use of hearing words, such as: 'I hear what you are saying', 'We'll discuss this further', 'I hear you loud and clear'

Kinaesthetic people are very physically orientated and like to move a lot. They have difficultly sitting for long periods and use lots of expressive gestures as they speak. Their style can be identified by their slow pace and use of action words, such as: 'It feels as if...', 'It slipped my mind', 'I have a solid grasp...'

Movements

» Matching and mirroring
When people have a strong connection with one another, they will subconsciously copy each other's body language. To quickly create a strong connection with the recruiter, the same technique may be applied.

As you are speaking with the recruiter, make a mental note of how they are sitting and what they are doing with their hands. Then, subtly mirror their position and gestures. If they are leaning forward, you might lean forward also. If they have their hands clasped on the table, you might do the same.

The key to successfully utilising this technique is subtlety. If we become obvious by reacting instantly to each and every change, the effectiveness of the technique will be lost. Similarly, if we mirror closed signals, we may accomplish only a negative connection.

The best time to mirror a position is when we engage in dialogue. For example: The recruiter leans forward as they begin to ask a question. As we engage our follow up response, a change in position would appear natural and go completely unnoticed.

» Leading
Leading is an influencing technique which can be used to judge the level of connection. For example: If you feel you have achieved rapport with the recruiter and both of you have your hands in your lap and are sat up straight, you could lean forward slightly and clasp your hands gently onto the table. If the recruiter follows your lead, you can be sure that you have established a strong connection.

Disconnection

It is important to be perceptive to signs that the recruiter has become disconnected so that we can be proactive in re-establishing a connection.

Before attempting to reconnect, however, it is important to establish the accuracy of our perceptions because we may have simply misread the signal or it could be a by-product of our paranoid imagination. Similarly, the perceived signal may be a momentary motion that has no substance or it may be unrelated to us entirely.

To reliably determine the accuracy of our observation, we first need to scan for clusters of signals that are supportive of our perception. If we observe two or more congruent signals, this is a definite cluster. Next, we can test our connection by attempting to 'lead' (see above). If the recruiter doesn't follow, this is also a sure sign that a disconnection has taken place.

Master the Art of Small Talk

Recruiters recognise that job interviews are nerve wracking events and will usually open the session with a brief period of small talk. Perhaps this is an attempt to merely break the ice, or possibly a way to judge your communication and people skills while under pressure. Either way, your involvement can have a direct impact on your overall success and consideration for your responses should be given.

To help you successfully navigate your way through the minefield of interview small talk, I have prepared the following guidelines.

» Stick to safe topics
  Keep your focus on positive or neutral topics such as the weather and traffic. Discussions about politics or religion should be avoided, as should negative or controversial current events. Each of these can stir up some very strong emotions and shift the interview in a negative direction very quickly.

» Show interest
  While discussions about the weather and traffic are not particularly engaging, an effort should be made to look interested.

» Give short responses
  Small talk should remain small. Long winded stories about the journey, the weather, or the latest sports news are not only unnecessary, they are also inappropriate. Respond in a conversational tone, but don't get carried away.

» Be sincere
  Being friendly too quickly or being overly complimentary may appear desperate and insincere. To be effective, keep pleasantries minimal and sincere.

Disconnection Signals

Signs of disconnection include:

» Fake smile
» Yawning
» Closed gestures
» Stretching
» Using barriers
» Shifting
» Directing their body away
» Tidying the desk
» Writing notes
» Slouching
» Fidgeting

Disapproval Signals

Signs of disapproval include:

» Pursed lips
» Frowning
» Eye squinting
» Jaw clenching
» Increased blinking rate
» Shaking head
» Licking lips
» Scratching
» Rubbing eyes

» Be positive
There is no room for negativity of any kind. Even if you had trouble finding the location or got stuck in a long traffic jam on your way to the venue, a positive response is the only one that should be considered. For instance:

"How was your journey?"
"Very well, thank you"

"I hope the traffic wasn't too terrible?"
"I expected a little traffic, so I left early for this reason"

"Did you find the venue okay?"
"Yes, thank you. I found your map to be a great help"

» Control your body language
Even during this seemingly informal discussion, our body language is important. Convey a professional and confident message by maintaining steady eye contact, keeping an upright posture and wearing a warm smile.

Plan an Exit Strategy

When the interview approaches its conclusion, regardless of what has happened and how we feel, it is important to depart gracefully for that final lasting impression.

Tip:

If a panel of recruiters are present, a handshake for each person is unnecessary. Simply thank the panel and shake hands with whomever escorts you to the door.

Note:

If the recruiter initiates a handshake, be sure to rise to a full standing position before taking their hand.

» Step 1: Gather your belongings
Before rising, gather your belongings and ensure a firm grip. If possible, leave your right hand free for the inevitable final handshake.

» Step 2: Straighten your clothing
As you rise from your seat, be sure to straighten up any disjointed attire such as your tie, jacket or skirt.

» Step 3: Exchange pleasantries
Once standing, smile and say "Thank you for taking the time to meet with me today". Then, if expected, exchange handshakes and make your way to the door.

» Step 4: Make your exit
Stop at the door, turn, smile and say a final "thank you". Then proceed with your exit and be sure to close the door behind you.

Journal Notes

Polish your Image

During the first few minutes of the interview, the recruitement team will make certain judgements about a candidates character and suitability based on their appearance. Thus, if we are to succeed in creating that all important positive first impression, it is essential that we make a valid effort to present a polished and conservative image.

To help you achieve this, I have prepared the following guidelines.

Organise your Outfit

Business casual may be perfectly acceptable for some airlines and it is the very least that should be considered. An acceptable minimum standard for casual business wear for women is no less than a reasonable length dress skirt or tailored trousers with a blouse or cardigan/sweater combination. For men, a collared shirt and trouser combination would apply.

For maximum impact, however, classic formal business attire is a safe choice that will give a clean, polished and professional appearance.

Whatever style of dress you ultimately choose, whether formal or informal, you need to pay attention to:

» Fit:
Wear clothing that fits your body correctly. Clothing that is too short or too long, too big or too small is never a good look.

» Suitability:
Even if you opt for a casual look, your attire needs to be suitable. Too much cleavage, exposed midriffs, and excessively short skirts are not suitable, so don't do it.

» Patterns:
Some patterns can appear overwhelming, so play it safe with a solid colour or stick to conservative and subtle patterns such as pinstripes.

» Colours:
Too much colour can also be overwhelming, so wear traditional colours, such as: navy blue, charcoal grey and black, and introduce colour sparingly and subtly through your shirt/blouse or tie. This will give your outfit a professional, yet unique character.

» Fabric:
Some fabrics wrinkle easily, so look for a suit that is made of a wrinkle resistant fabric such as wool.

Gents

Tie

» Select a tie colour that is conservative and a pattern that is subtle. Exuberant patterns or character ties should be avoided.

» For a strong and confident look opt for a larger knot, such as the Pratt or Windsor.

» The optimum length of a tie is one which falls to the same level as the belt buckle.

» Tie bars and clips may be worn to keep the tie in place.

Pratt Tie Knot   Double Windsor

Shirt

» Choose a good quality 100% cotton shirt which has long sleeves.

» Subtle patterns are generally acceptable, but avoid horizontal stripes.

» Select a colour which compliments your suit and contrasts your tie. White and blue are the most conservative choices.

» Cuff link style cuffs are fine, as are buttoned down styles.

Belt

Your belt must feature a conservative buckle and the strap should coordinate with the colour of your shoes.

Suit Style

» A well tailored suit in a wrinkle free fabric will create a sophisticated and professional image.

» Traditional colours, such as navy blue, black and charcoal grey are the most formal and professional.

» Solid colours or subtle patterns are acceptable choices.

» A matching jacket will create a professional and neat look, and build credibility.

» A well fitting suit jacket will button up easily without a significant tug across the fabric and the sleeves will allow the shirt cuffs to extend a 1/4 of an inch beyond the jacket cuffs when relaxed.

Socks

Socks should be dark and long enough to cover skin when seated. Mid-calf length is ideal for this purpose.

Shoes

Shoes should be clean and neat and in a style and colour which complements the overall look of the outfit.

Ladies

Blouse

» Choose a good quality and conservative blouse which has shoulders and sleeves.

» Avoid low cut necklines and button up at least two buttons up from the cleavage line.

» Subtle patterns are generally acceptable, but avoid horizontal stripes.

» Select a colour which compliments your suit. White and off white are the most conservative choices.

Suit Style

» A well tailored suit in a wrinkle free fabric will create a sophisticated and professional image.

» Traditional colours, such as navy blue, black and charcoal grey are the most formal and professional.

» Solid colours or subtle patterns are acceptable choices.

» A matching jacket will create a professional and neat look, and build credibility.

Skirt, Dress or Trousers

Skirts and dresses provide a more streamlined and feminine appearance, however, a trouser suit is an acceptable choice so you should proceed with your personal preference.

Skirts and dresses must be a conservative length that is no less than knee length.

Always opt for loose fit trousers, rather than tight fit.

Hosiery

For a sophisticated look, tights or stockings in a natural colour should be worn.

Shoes

Shoes should be clean and neat and in a style which complements the overall look of the outfit.

Closed court shoes in a low to medium heel are safe choices.

Tend to your Grooming

» Hands & Nails
Ensure that your nails are clean, neatly trimmed and reasonable in length. Nail polish should be conservative and match in colour. Avoid charms, glitter and multicoloured polish.

» Cosmetics
Use cosmetics to conceal blemishes and enhance your assets but avoid going over the top. Less is more in a formal interview setting where a natural and polished look will be appreciated.

» Hair
Hair should be neat and well groomed, and outrageous colours or styles should be avoided. Frizzy or loose ends can appear messy so should be brushed into place and fixed, but be careful not to produce a slicked down appearance.

Male cabin crew are not normally permitted to have beards so a cleanly shaven or closely trimmed style is recommended.

Accessorize

» Perfume & Cologne
If you choose to wear perfume or cologne, select a light scent and wear it sparingly.

» Jewellery
Keep jewellery minimal and conservative. Wear no more than one ring per hand and avoid oversized pieces.

» Watch
Wear a simple working watch which doesn't beep.

» Portfolio
Consider carrying a small leather portfolio rather than a briefcase or everyday handbag. Portfolios are simple, organised and easy to carry.

» Tattoos & Facial Piercings
Visible tattoos and facial piercings are not acceptable. Tattoos will need to be concealed and piercings. removed.

The Final Countdown

The Run Up

» Rehearse
On the final run up to the event, set aside some time to go through a final rehearsal of your presentation. Practice answering questions and going over talking points with a friend or relative and use this opportunity to iron out any wrinkles.

» Perform a dry run
If possible, take the opportunity to visit the venue in advance. This dry run will familiarise you with the route, parking and travel time and allow you to avoid becoming lost or late on the day. If you can do the route at the same time of day, you'll benefit from the added simulation of traffic and road conditions.

If you are unable to make an advance visit the venue, use the internet to map out a detailed route map that also provides distance and time estimations.

» Inspect your outfit
A few days before the event, take out the outfit you plan to wear and make sure it is clean, pressed, and has no buttons missing. Have it dry cleaned and repaired if necessary.

» Get a hair cut
Consider having your hair cut a week out from the day. This will allow the cut to soften slightly for a more natural look, while still retaining some of the freshness of the cut.

» Calm your nerves
If you feel your anxiety levels begin to escalate, put aside time to practice the strategies outlined on pages 31 through 45.

The Evening Before

» Review your résumé
As you complete a final review of your résumé, notice and take pride in your listed achievements. Take the time to remind yourself of why you want the job and what you have to offer.

» Check travel arrangements
If travelling by car, make sure the tank has plenty of petrol and that you have change available for parking meters. If using public transport, check timetables.

To keep your vocal cords sufficiently lubricated, you must keep hydrated.

Make sure you drink plenty of water 24 hours before the event.

Three litres of water per day is the ideal volume.

» **Prepare your outfit**
Take out the outfit you plan to wear and go through a final inspection to make sure it is clean and pressed. Inspect your hosiery for runs or holes. Clean and polish your shoes. Prepare your accessories and gather your portfolio pieces. Then, lay the pieces out ready for the morning.

» **Organise your portfolio**
To avoid a morning rush, prepare your portfolio in advance.

» **Get an early night**
To ensure you are fresh and alert, you'll need a good night's sleep. So, aim to retire no later than 11 pm. A warm aromatherapy bath before bed will help you relax and unwind.

» **Set your alarm**
Before winding down for the night, ensure your alarm is set to the appropriate time. For caution, you may set two alarms or enlist a relative to give you a friendly wake up call.

On the Day

» **Drink a glass of water**
As soon as you rise, rehydrate and wake up your system with a large glass of water.

» **Stretch**
Incorporating a full body stretch into your morning routine will increase blood flow and wake up your tired muscles.

» **Psyche yourself up**
Jump start your motivation by chanting your incantations, acknowledging your goals and visualising your success.

» **Listen to music**
Listening to your favourite upbeat music is a great way to put you in a good mood. It will lighten the atmosphere and increase your energy level.

» **Eat a good breakfast**
Oatmeal is light, natural and slow releasing so it will provide ample energy for the day. Perhaps combine it with a protein shake and piece of fruit for a power breakfast.

» **Leave with plenty of time to spare**
Arriving late to an interview means you immediately start the interview from behind the rest of the candidates. You also risk arriving in a panic. You should, therefore, aim to arrive at least 15 minutes early and allow extra travelling time to account for any unforeseen delays.

It is better to be an hour early than it is to be just a minute late. You can always grab a coffee and go through your notes.

Portfolio Essentials

Documentation
» Copies of your résumé
» Interview invitation
» A copy of your application form
» Passport
» Certificates
» Reference details

Photographs
You should take one full length with one or two passport sized.

A notepad
A notepad is tidier than lots of pieces of paper.

2 pens
With two pens, you will have a backup if the first runs out of ink or becomes lost. Alternatively, you can lend one to another candidate.

A pencil and eraser
These two items are a must as they will make any mistakes easy to rectify.

Smokers Beware!

Stale smoke will linger on your clothing for hours, so avoid smoking before or during the interview.

On Arrival

» Freshen up
If you have time, and it's convenient to do so, take a moment when you arrive to freshen up. Inspect your outfit, wash your hands, touch up your makeup, pop in a breath mint and spritz some deodorant. Be sure to discard any gum or breath mints before you enter the announce your arrival.

» Turn off your cell phone
To avoid potential interruptions, turn off your cell phone or put it on silent mode as soon as you arrive.

Journal Notes

Journal Notes

Part 3

Apply

....

Introduction
Write a Winning Cover Letter
Create a Compelling CV/Résumé
Prepare a Powerful Application
Produce Polished Photographs
Surpass the Telephone Screening
Concluding Notes

Introduction

Note:

If you have previously applied and been unsuccessful through the initial screening process, most airlines have a six to twelve month waiting period between re-applications.

Need Not Apply

If you plan to attend an open day, it may be unnecessary to apply beforehand. You should check this with the airline before proceeding.

There are several ways you can register your interest for a cabin crew position, these include:

» Traditional paper cover letter and résumé/application form combination

» Email cover letter with digital résumé/application form

» Online application facility

In recent years, many airlines have moved onto, and prefer, online application facilities. As a result, it would be wise to check with each airline before proceeding with any of the alternative methods. If, however, you don't have easy access to the internet it is generally acceptable to request a postal application pack or submit your résumé to the airline's recruitment office for consideration.

Whichever method you ultimately select, the following pages contain detailed guidance notes that will assist you with each format.

So, without further ado, let's proceed with this important section on applying...

Font Comparisons

Serif Fonts	
Font	Size
Arial	14
Arial	12
Arial	11
Arial	10
Verdana	14
Verdana	12
Verdana	11
Verdana	10

Sans Serif Fonts	
Font	Size
Georgia	14
Georgia	12
Georgia	11
Georgia	10
Garamond	14
Garamond	12
Garamond	11
Garamond	10

SansSerif

Serif

Write a Winning Cover Letter

A cover letter is a valuable opportunity to introduce yourself and highlight your suitability for the role. Use the guidelines below to ensure a strong first impression.

Appearance

» Paper
Keep to the standard paper size of your geographic location. In Europe, this is 210x297mm and in the United States, it is 8.5x11".

A quality uncoated paper, such as bond, linen and laid, is often used for corporate stationery and, as such, can give your letter an important feel. Don't be overly concerned with this aspect, though, as its significance is minimal.

» Decoration
Avoid decoration such as floral borders or marble background effects. Instead, add some character by using a personalised logo.

Jane Doe

» Length
One page is ideal. Any longer, and you risk losing the reader's interest

» Margins
Use acceptable business format margins of .75" to 1.0" left and right

» Spacing & Alignment
Your letter should be single spaced, flush left, with each paragraph separated by a blank line.

» Fonts
Use a popular font that is clear, easy to read and not overly decorative. Universal fonts such as Georgia, Arial and Verdana work well.

Use an adequate font size that is large enough that the reader doesn't have to squint, no less than 9 or 10 points, but not so large that the letter doesn't fit on the page, around 12 points.

Conventions

Addresses

» Return Address
Europe: Top centre or right-hand corner
America: Top left-hand corner

» Recipients Address
In Europe, the recipients address is placed at the left side of the page. Either on the same line as, or one line below, the date line. In America, it is placed two lines below the return address at the left side.

> Mr / Mrs / Ms / Miss ...
> Company
> Building Number, Street
> Address Line 2
> City
> State/County
> Zip/Post Code
> COUNTRY (in capital letters)

Date

» European format: 15 May 2008
Positioned on the right, one line below the return address.

» American format: May 15, 2008
Positioned at the top left-hand corner, above the return address.

Opening Salutation

A more favourable impression will be created if you make an effort to find out the name of the person who is accepting applications and then address him/her personally.

Use the title (Mr, Mrs, Miss or Ms) followed by the, correctly spelled, surname

» Dear Ms Loren

If, despite your best efforts, you cannot obtain the addressees name, use one of the following salutations:

» Dear Sir or Madam

» To whom it may concern

Closing Salutation

If you have addressed the recipient by name, your should conclude the letter with 'Yours sincerely', otherwise 'Yours faithfully' is appropriate.

Enclosures

As you will be enclosing your résumé or application form, you need to state their inclusion. You can either list all enclosed documents separately or just write 'Encl.' or 'Enclosures' below the signature line.

Attn

Sometimes the name of the addressee is preceded by attn (attention) or FAO (for the attention of), e.g. attn Ms Loren

Ms, Mrs or Miss

If you are writing to a woman and do not know if she uses Mrs or Miss, you can use Ms

Punctuation

In Britain, the salutation would be followed by either a comma, or no punctuation mark. In America, a colon is generally the accepted standard.

Proofread

As with any important document, absolutely no errors should be present. A typo, a poor printing job or a misspelling will create a poor impression.

Format

Cover letters should be written in standard business format and consist of a header, introduction, body and conclusion.

» Header
The header section consists of your return address, the date, recipients address and salutation.

» Introduction
The introduction explains your reason for contacting the airline. If you are responding to an advertisement, refer to it and the source that published it.

» Body
The body briefly highlights what you have to offer and why you are suitable for the position. Don't let modesty prevent you from mentioning your strengths and don't simply repeat your résumé. Simply summarise the most relevant aspects that address the airline's requirements directly..

You can also use the body of the letter to address gaps in your work history or other problems evident on your résumé. But do not draw attention to these unless you must, and never apologise. Always maintain a positive, confident tone.

» Conclusion
The conclusion sums up the letter and should be concise. Thank the reviewer, state your desire for an interview and indicate how you can be reached. If you intend to follow up with a phone call, state your intention to do so and then be sure you do it.

Going Digital

The fastest way to apply for employment is via email. However, with so much spam haunting our mailboxes it is also the fastest way to have your application trashed. To avoid being sent to the trash or spam box, stick to the simple guidelines that follow.

» Include an informative subject:
If you are responding to an advertisement, use the cited job title and job code. If you are making a speculative enquiry, put a few words stating your objective, for example: Jane Doe -- Résumé for Cabin Crew Position

» Send you résumé in the message body:
Paste a plain text version of your résumé right into the body of the message, immediately following your signature. This way, you avoid being automatically deleted by email systems that reject email attachments, and the recipient will have the benefit of seeing it as soon as he or she opens the message.

» Ensure proper email formatting
A hard return will sometimes produce two blank lines instead of the one intended. Take the time to make sure your email looks as good on all computers and in all email systems as it does on your screen.

With regards to the content and layout, much of the conventional cover letter guidelines apply, but with the obvious exceptions and following alterations:

» Signature Block:
Much of the information that would be included in a header will now become part of your signature. A signature is a block of text, consisting of your name and contact details, which is appended at the footer of your email message.

Signature blocks can be plain text or something fancier with images and colours, however, a complex signature can become illegible if the recipient has opted to receive email messages only in plain text format.

Prepared Phrases

Introduction

» I would like to express my strong interest in the position of (position) with (company)

» I am applying for the position of (position), which was advertised (date) in (source)

» (Name) informed me of an opening for (position) that is available at (company)

Body

» From my enclosed résumé, you will find that my experiences / skills / ... align perfectly with the requirements you have outlined for the position

» While my enclosed résumé provides a good overview of my experiences / skills / ... I have also listed some specific skills that meet your requirements for the position

» According to your advertisement, your position requires (skills). These skills I have developed during ... (experience).

» I have more than ... years of ... experience.

» I am very competent in ...

Conclusion

» I would welcome the opportunity to meet with you to discuss this position and my background in more detail

» If you would like to schedule an interview, or otherwise discuss my interest in this position, you can reach me via my mobile on (telephone number) or via email (email address).

» I will call you in a few days / next week / in early July / ... to discuss an interview.

» I look forward to talking with you.

» I look forward to hearing from you soon.

» Thank you for your time and consideration.

» Your consideration is greatly appreciated.

Jane Doe

16 Any Road • Any Where
Any Town • AN8 9SE
United Kingdom
+44 (0)4587 875848 • Jane.Doe@Anymail.com

Attn: Ms Loren   25 February 2011
Fly High Airlines
23, Airport Road
London
SW9 0DD
UNITED KINGDOM

Dear Ms Loren

I would like to express my strong interest in the position of cabin crew with Fly High Airlines, thus I have enclosed a copy of my résumé and photographs for your review and consideration.

As you will note, my enclosed résumé highlights my extensive eight years experience within the retail industry. Within which, I have built extensive customer relations, team working and supervisory experience, which have also greatly enhanced my communication and interpersonal skills.

With these skills and experiences combined with my passion for the airline industry, my motivation to succeed, strong attention to detail, and unparalleled work ethic, I am confident that I will make a positive contribution to the airline and excel as a member of the Fly High cabin crew team.

I would welcome the opportunity to meet with you to discuss this position and my background in more detail, and to explore the ways I could contribute to the ongoing success of your airline.

If you would like to schedule an interview, or otherwise discuss my interest in this position, you can reach me on +44 (0) 4587 875 848 or via email Jane.Doe@Anymail.com

Thank you for your time and consideration. I look forward to hearing from you.

Yours sincerely,

Jane Doe
Encl

Figure 3. Cover Letter Sample

Subject: Cabin Crew Opening - Reference: CC34873429

Dear Ms Loren

I would like to express my strong interest in the position of cabin crew with Fly High Airlines, thus I have attached a copy of my résumé and photographs for your review and consideration.

As you will note, my attached résumé highlights my extensive eight years experience within the retail industry. Within which, I have built extensive customer relations, team working and supervisory experience, which has also greatly enhanced my communication and interpersonal skills.

With these skills and experiences, combined with my passion for the airline industry, my motivation to succeed, strong attention to detail, and unparalleled work ethic, I am confident that I will make a positive contribution to the airline and excel as a member of the Fly High cabin crew team.

I would welcome the opportunity to meet with you to discuss this position and my background in more detail, and to explore the ways I could contribute to the ongoing success of your airline.

If you would like to schedule an interview, or otherwise discuss my interest in this position, you can reach me on +44 (0) 4587 875 848 or via email Jane.Doe@Anymail.com

Thank you for your time and consideration. I look forward to hearing from you.

Yours sincerely,
Jane Doe

Landline: +44 (0) 1577 385 927 | **Mobile:** +44 (0) 4587 875 848 | **Email:** Jane.Doe@Anymail.com
Address: 16 Any Road, Any Where , Any Town, AN8 9SE, UNITED KINGDOM

JANE DOE
16 Any Road • Any Where • Any Town • AN8 9SE • United Kingdom
+44 (0)4587 875848 • Jane.Doe@Anymail.com

OBJECTIVE
Seeking to pursue a cabin crew position with an airline that rewards commitment and hard work, and offers opportunities to progress.

KEY SKILLS

Communication Skills:
Exhibits exceptional written and verbal communication skills, and is adept at communicating effectively with people at all levels, and in a manner appropriate to the audience.

Interpersonal Ability:
Unsurpassed interpersonal skills with a proven ability to quickly develop and maintain relationships with customers and colleagues.
...

Figure 4. E-Cover Letter Sample

Journal Notes

Create a Compelling CV/Résumé

CV vs Résumé

The main difference between a résumé and CV (Curriculum Vitae) is in the length. A CV is much more comprehensive than a résumé, which is generally brief.

A curriculum vitae is more commonly used In Europe, Asia, Africa and the Middle East.

Note:

For the sake of consistency, I will refer to this document as a résumé from this point forward

First and foremost, a résumé is used to enable employers to screen out unsuitable candidates. If successful through this initial screening stage, it will then be used to formulate suitable questions for the interview.

Because the recruiters will have no information about you beyond this document, it will be a major influence in the nature and direction of the interview. This allows an element of predictability and makes it a very powerful document indeed.

With such a valuable tool at your disposal, it is important that it represents the best you have to offer. If your résumé is strong, it will focus the recruiter's questioning on information that presents your image strongly. The following guidelines will help you achieve this.

Appearance

To retain consistency, you should continue the theme used for your cover letter (See page 73). When viewed as an entire package, it will create a very professional and consistent image. The exceptions are:

» Colour
Use colour sparingly. Black text, with a consistent injection of colour for the headings will make your resume more pleasing to the human eye, but photocopying may be problematic.

» Length
For this type of position, one or two pages is ideal. However, don't be constrained by this advice if doing so will mean that you have to squeeze your data in and use a tiny 8 point font, If you do find your résumé going beyond this quota, be sure that it isn't being filled with unnecessary, unfocused or excessive detail.

» Verso Printing
Double sided prints are harder to photocopy and risk show through. Stick to single sided prints for a cleaner look.

» Staples
Never staple your sheets together. Staples are inconvenient for the employer if they need to photocopy or scan your résumé, plus the reviewer may want to view the pages side by side. A traditional paper clip is acceptable.

» Identification
Be sure all of the pages include your name and page numbers so they can be easily reconnected should they become separated.

OCR Technology

To facilitate more efficient processing of résumés, some larger airlines use a computerised tracking system. This system uses OCR (Optical Character Recognition) technology whereby incoming résumés are scanned as a graphic image, converted back into text, read and added to the database.

With this in mind, it is important to write and format your résumé in such a way that it can be successfully processed by these sophisticated systems. In this instance, the following guidelines apply:

Formatting
Simple formatting will yield the best results. So, avoid unnecessary and unreliable formatting such as italics, shading, and fancy fonts and stick to a simple one column, table less design using a standard typeface such as Georgia, Arial or Verdana.

Keywords
The system scans your résumé for keywords that indicate your skills, qualifications and experience. Following the scan, a score will be awarded based on the number of 'hits'. From this score, the system will either generate a letter of invitation, or a letter of rejection.

To ensure a high score, and an invitation letter, it is essential that you learn and inject as many keywords as possible throughout your resume. The following highlighted keywords are the most widely scanned for:

» Good **communication** and **interpersonal** skills

» A **confident** and **friendly** personality

» Extensive **customer** service experience

» **Confidence** in dealing with a range of **people**

» The ability to work effectively in a **team**

» **Numeracy** skills for handling transactions

» Ability to handle **difficult customers** firmly and politely

» Ability to stay **calm**, **composed** and **focused** under **pressure**

» The ability to be **tactful** and **diplomatic**, but also **assertive** when necessary

Action Verbs

Action verbs express action. They are positive, powerful and directive, and should be used abundantly throughout your résumé.

Here are just a few examples:

» Communicated
» Conveyed
» Directed
» Explained
» Expressed
» Incorporated
» Interacted
» Listened
» Participated
» Persuaded
» Resolved
» Suggested
» Arranged
» Assisted
» Guided
» Provided
» Handled
» Generated
» Improved
» Trained

Consider the following sentence: "As a hairdresser I had to carry out consultations with clients, which involved providing advice"

Now notice how using direct action verbs makes the sentence much more powerful: "As a hairdresser, I **consulted** with clients and **provided advice**"

A full list of action verbs can be found on page 101

Format

There are three basic résumé formats:

» Chronological:
The chronological résumé highlights the dates, places of employment and job titles, and is most effective for candidates who have a strong, solid work history. It is less effective for those who want to disguise gaps in employment or frequent job changes.

» Functional:
A functional résumé focuses on skills and experience rather than work history. Its ability to accentuate your transferable skills and detract attention from your career history makes it better suited to those who want to downplay an extreme career change or a chequered employment history. This style is less useful if you have limited work experience as there will be little to highlight.

» Combination:
The combination résumé, as the name implies, is a combination of the chronological and functional formats. It highlights both your work history and your transferable skills, and is most effective when you have a great deal of transferable skills and a solid work history.

The chronological format is most preferred by employers, followed closely by the combination format. The functional format is the least effective.

Outline

For the purpose of a cabin crew position, I have listed possible résumé sections below, in suggested order:

Applicant Information

At the beginning of the résumé, include your name, your home mailing address, your telephone number(s), and your e-mail address. If you have both temporary and permanent addresses, include them both.

Objective Statement (Optional)

An objective is a short statement which defines your career goals. It gives your résumé focus and shows that you have given consideration to your career direction.

Examples: Seeking to utilise extensive customer service experience and exceptional communicative ability within a cabin crew role.

Seeking to pursue a cabin crew position with an airline that rewards commitment and hard work, and offers opportunities to progress.

Key Skills (Optional)

The key skills section provides a fantastic opportunity for you to quickly express your suitability for the role and show what transferable skills your will bring to the position. Additionally, it will bulk out your résumé with the keywords needed for OCR scanning technology (See page 82).

Key skills to consider are: Communication Skills
Interpersonal Ability
Customer Focus
Team Player
Problem Solver
Leadership

Employment History (Chronological & Combination Formats)

Your employment history should be displayed in reverse chronological order, that is starting with your most recent position and working backwards, and include: the name of the organisation, the position held, the period of employment, the duties performed and results achieved.

The period of employment should include both the start and end dates, and can consist of only the month and year.

Tip:

If you include an objective, focus your attention on what you can do for the employer, not what the employer can do for you.

Note:

While an objective is optional, it is important if you are changing fields, are a graduate or an entry-level job seeker, or have a diverse employment history.

Tip:

Don't limit your key skills to those gained through work experience. Consider skills you have gained from your hobbies, during studies, and voluntary placements.

Note:

Employment
Employment history is a broad term that can include relevant internships, summer or seasonal jobs, part time work, and voluntary placements. This is especially important if you have little paid experience.

Notes:

A Team Effort
If any of your achievements were the direct result of a team effort, point this out as it will show team spirit.

Promotions
Don't forget to mention any promotions or increases in responsibility.

Quick Tip

If you have gaps in your employment history, say what you were doing during this time. For example: Bringing up children, travelling,

Languages

If you have more than one language ability, indicate whether you speak, read, and/or write the language, and include the level to which you are proficient, such as: native, fluent, proficient or basic conversational ability.

References

Unless specifically requested, the inclusion of reference information is completely optional.

When listing your references, be sure to include: Name, title, professional relationship to you (e.g., Supervisor, manager, and team leader), telephone number and mailing address.

If you decide not to include details, a simple statement such as "References are available on request" is sufficient.

When describing your duties use action phrases, rather than compete sentences or generic job descriptions, and list any accomplishments which back up any key skill statements that you have made. For example, if you have stated 'extensive leadership experience' you can use a short action statement such as: "Supervised and trained a team of four junior-level stylists". Three to five of these statements are ideal.

If some entries are more relevant to the cabin crew position, emphasise these and provide only summaries for those of less significance.

Education Summary
Starting with the most recent and working backwards, include the schools/colleges/universities you have attended. Within each entry, include the year of completion ("In progress" or "expected" are acceptable, if necessary) and award(s) you achieved.

Certifications (Optional)
If you have attended any formal certification courses, e.g., First aid, life saving, then list the details here noting the institution name, date and certification awarded.

Activities and Interests (Optional)
Recreational interests reveal a great deal about your personality and create depth to your character. They also serve as excellent sources of additional skills and experiences, which can be advantageous if you lack certain skills and/or experience.

Generalised list statements such as: 'reading, watching television, sport and socialising' are not only bland, they are also too common. Additionally, a statement such as: 'I enjoy spending time with my mates, hitting the town and going out on the razz" lacks variety, doesn't highlight any key skills, and sounds very unprofessional.

Instead, use something such as: 'I have been a keen footballer for as long as I can remember and am an active member of Anytown women's football club where I have been captain of the team for 3 years. I have an active interest in nature, and regularly get involved with and manage conservation assignments. To relax, I attend yoga and meditation classes, which help to keep me focused and relieve stress.'

This statement gives an immediate impression of someone who is balanced and committed. Their interests highlight several admirable qualities such as team spirit and leadership, and it also details their methods of stress management. A recruitment officer would form a positive impression of the candidate based on a statement such as this.

Jane Doe

Seeking to pursue a cabin crew position with an airline that rewards commitment and hard work, and offers opportunities to progress.

Key Skills

Communication Skills
Exhibits exceptional written and verbal communication skills, and is adept at communicating effectively with people at all levels, and in a manner appropriate to the audience.

Interpersonal Ability
Unsurpassed interpersonal skills with a proven ability to quickly develop and maintain relationships with customers and colleagues.

Customer Focus
Experienced at providing a high quality service to customers at all levels, and skilled at effectively dealing with and resolving complaints.

Team Spirited
Skilled team player who adapts quickly to different team dynamics and excels at building trusting relationships with colleagues at all levels.

Problem Solver
Creative thinker who applies logic and initiative to difficult situations.

Employment History

Freelance Hairdresser   **Feb '03 - Present**
- » Manage and maintain a customer base of over 100 clients
- » Consult and advise customers
- » Ensure customer satisfaction
- » Provide a friendly and professional service
- » Maintain up to date records and accounts

Trina's Hair Salon | Senior Stylist   **Aug '00 – Feb '03**
- » Supervised and trained a team of four junior-level stylists
- » Hired work experience students
- » Consulted and advised customers
- » Ensured customer comfort and satisfaction
- » Provided a friendly and professional service

16 Any Road • Any Where
Any Town • AN8 9SE
United Kingdom

+44 (0)4587 875848
Jane.Doe@Anymail.com

Figure 5. Sample Combination Résumé Page 1

Jane Doe

Continued from page 1...

My confident and
friendly nature
will enable me to
fit in and
complement
your existing team

Employment History

Trina's Hair Salon - Junior Stylist   **April '98 – Aug '00**

» Consulted and advised customers
» Ensured customer comfort and satisfaction
» Provided a friendly and professional service

Macey's Hair Salon - Receptionist   **July '96 – April '98**

» Delivered the highest level of customer service
» Ensured customer comfort
» Provided a friendly and professional service
» Assisted with enquiries and resolved complaints

Education Summary

Any College (2001)	NVQ 3 - Hairdressing
Any College (1999)	NVQ 2 - Hairdressing
Any College (1998)	NVQ 1 – Hairdressing
Any High School (1996)	11 GCSE's (grade A–D)

Certifications

British Red Cross   Basic First Aid – Sept '06

Languages

Fluent in spoken and written Spanish
Basic conversational ability in French

Activities & Interests

I have been a keen footballer for as long as I can remember and
am an active member of Any Town women's football club where I
have been captain of the team for 3 years. I have an active interest
in nature and regularly get involved with and manage conservation
assignments. To relax, I attend yoga and meditation classes that help
to keep me focused and relieve stress.

16 Any Road • Any Where
Any Town • AN8 9SE
United Kingdom

+44 (0)4587 875848
Jane.Doe@Anymail.com

References

Written references are available on request

Figure 6. Sample Combination Résumé Page 2

Going Digital

Résumés can be formatted for digital distribution by using a universally friendly format such as:

Plain Text Format (.txt)
Plain text format is the simplest of the three formats. As the name suggests, it is stripped of virtually all of its formatting and, as a result, is not particularly visually appealing. Functionality wise it is without limitations as it is completely cross compatible and virus free. You can attach it to an email, embed it within the body of an email message, or use it to cut and paste into online forms.

To create a .txt file, simply open your résumé in a word processing program . Save the file using 'Save as' and select file type: Text only (*.txt).

Rich Text Format (.rtf)
Rich text résumés can be created using word processing software, such as Microsoft Word, and saved as .rtf format. The formatting within this style is much more visually pleasing than the plain text format, however, complex formatting may look strange when opened in different software on different computers. The solution is to keep it simple by avoiding unusual fonts and excessive formatting.

This format works well as an attachment when accompanied by a text version that is pasted within the e-cover letter.

Portable Document Format (.pdf)
The PDF format is probably the most versatile format of the three as it is completely cross compatible, virus free, and retains all its original formatting regardless of the computer it is viewed on. As such, it has a clean and professional appearance.

You can convert your word processed résumé into a PDF document by using the following software:

» OpenOffice Writer

» Microsoft Office Word

» Cute PDF Writer

» PDF Creator

Note:

Before proceeding with any one format, you should note that some email systems will automatically reject e-mails that contain attachments. So, proceed with caution.

Sending your résumé via email
You can send your résumé by embedding it within the text of the email or attaching it as an external attachment.

To embed your résumé within the email message, simply copy and paste it into the body of the message.

If, however, you intend to send your résumé as an email attachment the following guidelines should be followed:

» Use your name, or some variation, as the filename. For instance: "janedoe-resume.pdf" or "j.doe.pdf"

» Avoid password protection

» Test, test and test again. Send it to a friend or two first to make sure it works as it should

JANE DOE
16 Any Road • Any Where • Any Town • AN8 9SE • United Kingdom
+44 (0)4587 875848 • Jane.Doe@Anymail.com

OBJECTIVE
Seeking to pursue a cabin crew position with an airline that rewards commitment and hard work, and offers opportunities to progress.

KEY SKILLS

Communication Skills:
Exhibits exceptional written and verbal communication skills, and is adept at communicating effectively with people at all levels, and in a manner appropriate to the audience.

Interpersonal Ability:
Unsurpassed interpersonal skills with a proven ability to quickly develop and maintain relationships with customers and colleagues.

Customer Focus:
Experienced at providing a high quality service to customers at all levels, and skilled at effectively dealing with and resolving complaints.

Team Player:
Skilled team player who adapts quickly to different team dynamics and excels at building trusting relationships with colleagues at all levels.

Problem Solver:
Creative thinker who applies logic and initiative to difficult situations.

...

Figure 7. Plain Text Résumé Sample

Journal Notes

Prepare a Powerful Application

Job applications are primarily used to collect data from potential applicants for the purpose of evaluating their skills, qualifications, employment history and motives. Unlike résumés, which are unique to each individual, its standardised format allows selectors to quickly peruse each form and screen out any unsuitable candidates.

From the airline's perspective, the form also serves a number of other purposes. Namely: To evaluate the applicant's literacy, ability to follow instructions, penmanship and communication skills. Selection to be interviewed can be extremely competitive so recruiters will be looking or any excuse to thin the pack. A careless applicant, or one who doesn't follow instructions, will quickly disqualify themselves.

Quick Tips

Before you Begin

» Photocopy the blank form

» Read through the form to familiarise yourself with the questions and any specific instructions

» Gather materials: Black pens, a pencil and eraser

» Gather the necessary information:
Personal details: Passport, contact information, vital statistics
Education and training information: Qualifications, dates, results
Employment History: Names, addresses, key dates

» Plan what you want to write in each section, taking note of the space available

» Practice on the photocopied forms, or use blank sheets of paper

» Walk away for a few hours and return with a fresh pair of eyes

» Proofread and make any necessary adjustments: Be mindful of typos, grammatical errors and inaccuracies

Completing the Form

- » Set aside sufficient time and minimise distractions
- » Follow instructions
- » Use black ink
- » Write clearly and neatly: Block capitals are tidy and easy to read
- » Keep your text within the space provided
- » Answer every question and use 'Not Applicable' or 'N/A' where questions are not relevant to you
- » Keep the tone positive and don't volunteer negative information
- » Be concise
- » Avoid continuations on separate sheets of paper if you can. If unavoidable, remember to clearly state your name and detail which part of the application form it is linked to

Finishing Off

- » Complete a final proofread
- » Make a copy of the final form for future reference
- » Select an envelope that is large enough not to require any folding of the form
- » Address the envelope correctly and apply the correct postage
- » Send it off before the closing date

Guidance Notes

Employment History

Unless requested otherwise, your employment history should be displayed in reverse chronological order, that is starting with your most recent position and working backwards,

When describing your duties (as noted on page 84) three to five action phrases have a better impact than complete sentences or generic job descriptions. Consider the following examples:

- » 'As a call centre officer, I answer customer queries and complaints over the telephone'
- » 'Addressed customer queries and resolved complaints'

The former example has a passive tone and is unnecessarily wordy. The latter example, on the other hand, still uses the important key words, but uses an active and punchy tone.

Faux Pas Alert

Consider the following examples.

> I CURRENTLY WORK AS A FREELANCE HAIRDRESSER AND HAVE WORKED IN CLIENT FACING ROLES FOR MORE THAN 8 YEARS. I AM LOOKING FOR A CHANGE IN MY LIFE DIRECTION AND FEEL THAT A CAREER AS CABIN CREW WILL GIVE ME THIS.

> I curently work as freelance hairdresser & have worked in client facing roles fore more than 8 years. I am looking for a change in my life direction and feel that that a career as cabin crew will give me this.

The first example is tidy and creates an positive impression of the candidate. Meanwhile, the second example is messy, full of typos and barely legible. It is clear that the candidate jumped straight in without planning. Hardly a positive first impression.

Note:

Due to the self explanatory nature of the majority of questions, only those that require additional guidance will be elaborated on further.

Past or Present Tense?

If it was a previous job, then use the past tense (initiat**ed**, facilitat**ed**, answer**ed**). If it is a current position, then use the present tense (assist, identify, create).

Most importantly, you must communicate your suitability for the position clearly by highlighting the skills and experience that are relevant and transferable. For example, a salon receptionist may include the following:

> Delivered the highest level of customer service
> Ensured customer comfort
> Provided a friendly and professional service
> Assisted with enquiries and resolved complaints

This active statement identifies customer contact experience, as well as other specific responsibilities and attributes that are required of cabin crew. It would be clear to any airline that this candidate has the necessary experience and is clearly suited for the position.

» Irrelevant positions
Where a position holds little or no relevance, short summaries are acceptable. If those positions were very brief, dated, or only part time, you may be able to safely exclude their inclusion altogether. You should only do so, however, if doing so will not create damaging gaps.

» Lack of relative experience
Most airlines will require some form of experience in a customer facing role. So if you lack experience, you should certainly get some. Whether you take on a short term voluntary post at a local charity shop or some weekend bar work, you will surely strengthen your application.

» Fragmented work history
A fragmented job history, one that is made up of lots of short-term jobs, will not present a favourable impression to a potential employer. Fortunately, there are several options you can consider which will minimise its impact:

> A process of elimination
> If eliminating brief, dated, irrelevant, or part time jobs will not create damaging gaps, you should consider doing so

> Spring into summer
> Instead of listing specific dates for summer jobs, you can simply state Summer 20xx to Spring 20xx.

> Consecutive combining
> Where several similar consecutive jobs appear, you can combine them into one chunk, for example:

> 2004–2006   Receptionist
> Aztec Hotel & Spa, Bloomfields Leisure,
> Trina's Hair & Beauty Salon

» Gaps in employment
If you have gaps in your employment history, you may be asked to elaborate on these. Whatever your reasons: maternity leave, study or travel break, be honest and positive, and be prepared to discuss the details openly.

If you were doing anything during the gaps, paid or unpaid, it would be ideal to insert them into your work history to fill the gaps.

For example:
2005–2009   Full Time Parent
Summer 2004–Spring 2005   Travelled around Europe

» Career progression
If you have remained with an employer for several years but have progressed through the ranks, you can make your progression more obvious by listing each position as you would a new job.

» Reasons for leaving
While your reason for leaving your current employment is probably for career advancement, you should consider expanding on this, if space permits, to make it more memorable. For example:

"To advance my career as cabin crew with an airline that I admire"

Your reasons for leaving your previous employment may be for any reason: career advancement, not enough hours, wider responsibilities, temporary contract, redundancy, maternity leave, study break, travel break, or company relocation. Whatever your reason, remain positive and avoid phrases such as fired, terminated, quit, illness and personal reasons,

If you were fired or quit under less than favourable conditions, avoid drawing attention to the fact by using neutral phrases such as 'job ended'. Alternatively, you can simply state 'Will explain at the interview'. Both of these will provide you with the opportunity to discuss the details openly at interview where you can create a more favourable and detailed response.

Remember, you should not lie about your reasons for leaving previous employment posts as they are grounds for dismissal in the future.

Awards

Outstanding excellence will show commitment and talent, so if you have achieved any awards through your activities, be sure to list them. Make sure the achievements are recent, though, as outdated awards may give the impression that you haven't achieved anything since.

Stretching the Truth

Don't be tempted to just tell them what you think they want to hear. Exaggerations or untruths can come back to haunt you if you're are quizzed about them at the interview, or even later in employment. Be equally mindful about over indulging as the recruiter may get the impression that your hobbies will take priority over your work.

Balancing Act

To achieve balance, list a mix of individual pursuits and group activities.

Leisure Interests

As noted on page 85, recreational interests create depth and humanises your character. A targeted list, which focuses on relevant skills, will form an immediate and positive impression. They also serve as excellent sources of additional skills and experiences, which can be advantageous if you lack employment experience.

Generalised list statements such as: 'reading, watching television, sport and socialising' should be avoided, as should unprofessional statements such as: 'I enjoy spending time with my mates, hitting the town and going out on the razz".

To enhance your application form positively, focus and expand on those interests that have some relevance to the position. For instance, being captain of a football team demonstrates leadership qualities, while volunteering at a local charity indicates good people skills.

Here is an example: 'I have been a keen footballer for as long as I can remember and am an active member of Any Town women's football club where I have been captain of the team for 3 years. I have an active interest in nature, and regularly get involved with and manage conservation assignments. To relax, I attend yoga and meditation classes, which help to keep me focused and relieve stress.'

This statement gives an immediate impression of someone who is balanced and committed. Their interests highlight several admirable qualities such as team spirit and leadership, and it also details their methods of stress management. A recruitment office would form a positive impression of the candidate based on a statement such as this.

References

Always get permission from the person(s) you state as your referee(s) and give them a copy of your application form or résumé to help them write a relevant reference that highlights your most important points.

If you don't have any work references that you can use, you should provide a character reference instead. This can be a school teacher, university lecturer or a friend in an authoritative position such as a police officer or doctor.

If you have been fired, or you resigned under less than favourable circumstances, you may want to call the employer to find out what they would say in response to reference checks. Usually, past employers will agree to use the term 'resigned' if you explain that your termination is hurting your chances of finding employment.

Additional Information / Personal Statement

At the end of most application forms, you will be presented with some form of additional information box. This box may simply state 'Additional Information',or it could be more specific, such as:

» Please state your reason for applying and why you feel you are suited to the position of cabin crew?

» Please provide further information which you feel will benefit your application

Essentially, this is an opportunity to sell yourself and you should use it to provide a power statement which summarises your experience, highlights your key skills, and shares your motives all within a few short paragraphs.

Consider the following example:

'As you will note, I have eight years experience within the retail industry. Within which, I have built extensive customer relations, team working and supervisory experience, which has also greatly enhanced my communication and interpersonal skills.

With these skills and experiences, combined with my passion for the airline industry, my motivation to succeed, strong attention to detail, and unparalleled work ethic, I am confident that I will make a positive contribution to the airline and excel as a member of the Fly High cabin crew team.

I would welcome the opportunity to meet with you to discuss this position and my background in more detail, and to explore the ways I could contribute to the ongoing success of your airline.'

The above example is concise. It focuses on what the candidate can offer the airline, rather than what the airline can offer the candidate, and it showcases skills and experiences that are an asset for a cabin crew position.

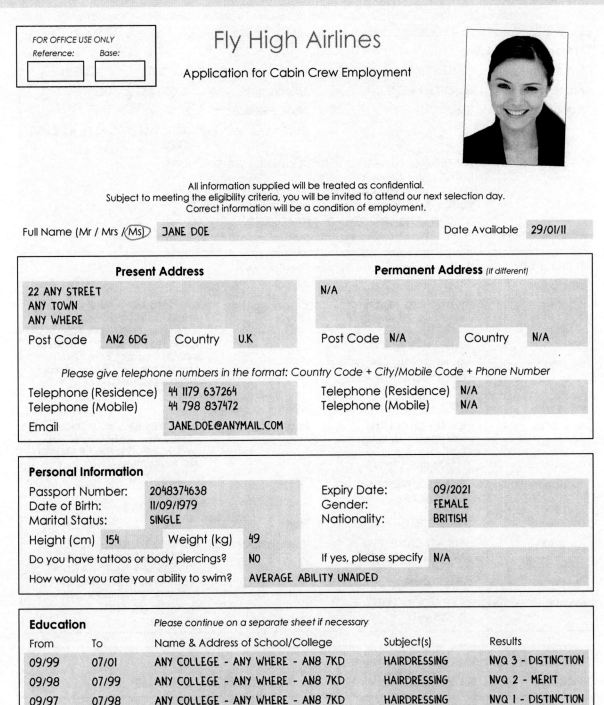

Fly High Airlines

Application for Cabin Crew Employment

FOR OFFICE USE ONLY
Reference: Base:

All information supplied will be treated as confidential.
Subject to meeting the eligibility criteria, you will be invited to attend our next selection day.
Correct information will be a condition of employment.

Full Name (Mr / Mrs /(Ms))   JANE DOE   Date Available   29/01/11

Present Address

22 ANY STREET
ANY TOWN
ANY WHERE

Post Code   AN2 6DG   Country   U.K

Permanent Address (If different)

N/A

Post Code   N/A   Country   N/A

Please give telephone numbers in the format: Country Code + City/Mobile Code + Phone Number

Telephone (Residence)   44 1179 637264
Telephone (Mobile)   44 798 837472
Email   JANE.DOE@ANYMAIL.COM

Telephone (Residence)   N/A
Telephone (Mobile)   N/A

Personal Information

Passport Number: 2048374638   Expiry Date: 09/2021
Date of Birth: 11/09/1979   Gender: FEMALE
Marital Status: SINGLE   Nationality: BRITISH

Height (cm)   154   Weight (kg)   49

Do you have tattoos or body piercings?   NO   If yes, please specify   N/A

How would you rate your ability to swim?   AVERAGE ABILITY UNAIDED

Education   *Please continue on a separate sheet if necessary*

From	To	Name & Address of School/College	Subject(s)	Results
09/99	07/01	ANY COLLEGE - ANY WHERE - AN8 7KD	HAIRDRESSING	NVQ 3 - DISTINCTION
09/98	07/99	ANY COLLEGE - ANY WHERE - AN8 7KD	HAIRDRESSING	NVQ 2 - MERIT
09/97	07/98	ANY COLLEGE - ANY WHERE - AN8 7KD	HAIRDRESSING	NVQ 1 - DISTINCTION
09/91	07/96	ANY SCHOOL - ANY WHERE - AN8 375	ENGLISH / GEOGRAPHY FRENCH / ART / CDT MATHS / SCIENCE / MATHS	8 GCSE'S GRADE A-C

Figure 8. Sample Application Form - Page 1

Present/Last Employer

Employer: SELF EMPLOYED   From: 01/02/03   To: PRESENT
Position: HAIRDRESSER   Salary: 15,000 PA
Address: N/A   Notice Required: NONE
                                       Reason for Leaving: TO PURSUE A CAREER AS CABIN
                                                            CREW

Responsibilities: MANAGE AND MAINTAIN A CUSTOMER BASE OF OVER 100 CLIENTS
                    CONSULT AND ADVISE CUSTOMERS
                    ENSURE CUSTOMER SATISFACTION
                    PROVIDE A FRIENDLY AND PROFESSIONAL SERVICE
                    MAINTAIN UP TO DATE RECORDS AND ACCOUNTS

Previous Employment   *Please continue on a separate sheet if necessary*

Employer: TRINA'S HAIR SALON   From: 16/02/00   To: 01/02/03
Address: 159 ANY CITY CENTRE   Responsibilities: SUPERVISED AND TRAINED A TEAM
              ANY TOWN - AN9 6DJ   OF FOUR JUNIOR-LEVEL STYLISTS -
                                                           HIRED WORK EXPERIENCE STUDENTS -
Position   SENIOR HAIR STYLIST   CONSULTED AND ADVISED CUSTOMERS
Reason for Leaving: TO PURSUE FREELANCE   - ENSURED CUSTOMER COMFORT AND
                     OPPORTUNITY   SATISFACTION - PROVIDED A FRIENDLY
                                                           AND PROFESSIONAL SERVICE

Employer: TRINA'S HAIR SALON   From: 05/04/98   To: 16/08/00
Address: 159 ANY CITY CENTRE   Responsibilities: CONSULTED AND ADVISED CUSTOMERS
              ANY TOWN - AN9 6DJ   - ENSURED CUSTOMER COMFORT AND
                                                           SATISFACTION - PROVIDED A FRIENDLY
Position   JUNIOR HAIR STYLIST   AND PROFESSIONAL SERVICE
Reason for Leaving: TO PURSUE PROMOTION
                     OPPORTUNITY

Employer: MACEY'S HAIR SALON   From: 24/07/97   To: 05/04/98
Address: 378 ANY CITY CENTRE   Responsibilities: DELIVERED THE HIGHEST LEVEL
              ANY TOWN - AN5 6SJ   OF CUSTOMER SERVICE - ENSURED
                                                           CUSTOMER COMFORT - PROVIDED A
Position   RECEPTIONIST   FRIENDLY AND PROFESSIONAL SERVICE
Reason for Leaving: TO PURSUE PROMOTION   - ASSISTED WITH ENQUIRIES AND
                     OPPORTUNITY   RESOLVED COMPLAINTS

Please explain any gaps in unemployment

UPON LEAVING SCHOOL IN 1996, I SPENT A YEAR TRAVELLING BEFORE MOVING INTO EMPLOYMENT

Please list any voluntary work

FOR THE LAST THREE YEARS, I HAVE VOLUNTEERED AT THE SAMARITANS HOMELESS SHELTER DURING THE CHRISTMAS
PERIOD, WHERE I HELP COOK AND SERVE BEVERAGES

Figure 9. Sample Application Form - Page 2

Additional Training

Give details of any first aid and/or nursing qualifications

BRITISH RED CROSS - BASIC FIRST AID TRAINING - 09/2006

Give details of languages spoken and abilities

ENGLISH - NATIVE LANGUAGE
FRENCH - READ, WRITE AND SPEAK FLUENTLY
SPANISH - BASIC CONVERSATIONAL ABILITY

Give details of any other training

I HAVE ATTENDED, AND PASSED, SHORT COURSES IN LEADERSHIP AND COMMUNICATION

Hobbies/Outside Interests

I HAVE BEEN A KEEN FOOTBALLER FOR AS LONG AS I CAN REMEMBER AND AM AN ACTIVE MEMBER OF ANY TOWN WOMEN'S FOOTBALL CLUB WHERE I HAVE BEEN CAPTAIN OF THE TEAM FOR 3 YEARS. I HAVE AN ACTIVE INTEREST IN NATURE AND REGULARLY GET INVOLVED WITH AND MANAGE CONSERVATION ASSIGNMENTS. TO RELAX, I ATTEND YOGA AND MEDITATION CLASSES THAT HELP TO KEEP ME FOCUSED AND RELIEVE STRESS.

Use the following space to provide any further information that you feel will benefit your application

AS YOU WILL NOTE, I HAVE AN EXTENSIVE EIGHT YEARS EXPERIENCE WITHIN THE RETAIL INDUSTRY. WITHIN THESE ROLES, I HAVE BUILT EXTENSIVE CUSTOMER RELATIONS, TEAM WORKING AND SUPERVISORY EXPERIENCE, AND GREATLY ENHANCED MY COMMUNICATION AND INTERPERSONAL SKILLS.

WITH THESE SKILLS AND EXPERIENCES, COMBINED WITH MY PASSION FOR THE AIRLINE INDUSTRY, MY MOTIVATION TO SUCCEED, STRONG ATTENTION TO DETAIL, AND UNPARALLELED WORK ETHIC, I AM CONFIDENT THAT I WILL MAKE A POSITIVE CONTRIBUTION TO THE AIRLINE AND EXCEL AS A MEMBER OF THE FLY HIGH CABIN CREW TEAM.

Declaration

Have you ever been convicted of a criminal offence which, at the date of application, is not a spent conviction as defined in the Rehabilitation of Offenders Act 1974?   Yes/No
If yes, then such convictions must be disclosed below.

N/A

Have you ever been refused entry, or deported from a foreign country?   Yes/No
If yes, please provide further details.

N/A

The details provided on this application are correct to my knowledge and belief. I understand that my application may be rejected or that I may be dismissed for withholding relevant information or giving false information. I am aware that my employment with Fly High Airlines will be subject to satisfactory references, medical form and criminal record checks.

Signature   Date   05/01/2011

Figure 10.   Sample Application Form - Page 3

Going Digital

The only significant difference between a digital application form and its paper counterpart is how they are completed. The questions will be similar and both require the same effort. Before you proceed, here are some useful pointers for you to follow:

» Be prepared
Before you proceed with the online form, have an up to date résumé to hand so that you have relevant details in front of you for reference.

» Offline drafting
The benefit of using a word processing package to draft and save you answers is threefold. Firstly, you will have a back up if any problems occur with the online form. Secondly, you will be able to run a spell check before you copy the information into the online system. Thirdly, your information will not be lost if your session times out (See the note below).

» Follow the instructions
The online system should guide you through the process, so follow any instructions carefully. In most cases there will be a help button if you get really stuck.

» Keep a record
Most online forms offer the option of storing your application for later completion or revision. If you choose to do this, be sure to keep a record of any user names and passwords so that you can sign back in.

» Time out
Some online application forms have a time out facility, whereby the session will close after a period of inactivity. If a system such as this is in place, there will usually be a timer displayed. However, this may not always be the case so you should always save your progress.

» Submission
Don't press the submit button until you have backed up your answers, proofread the application form and are 100% happy with your entries. Once it has been submitted, you can't reverse the submission.

Preparation Essentials

Personal Information
» Passport
» Contact information (telephone number, email, fax)
» Personal statistics (height, weight)

Education and Training Details
» Names and addresses of institutions
» Qualifications and results
» Dates

Career History
» Names of employers
» Dates
» Reference details

Action Verbs

Achieved	Enlisted	Organised
Addressed	Established	Originated
Advocated	Evaluated	Overhauled
Allocated	Examined	Oversaw
Analysed	Executed	Performed
Anticipated	Expedited	Persuaded
Appraised	Fabricated	Pioneered
Approved	Facilitated	Planned
Arbitrated	Forecasted	Presented
Arranged	Formulated	Produced
Assembled	Founded	Projected
Assessed	Generated	Promoted
Attained	Guided	Publicised
Authored	Handled	Recommended
Balanced	Identified	Recruited
Budgeted	Illustrated	Reduced
Built	Implemented	Referred
Calculated	Improved	Repaired
Catalogued	Increased	Reported
Clarified	Influenced	Represented
Classified	Informed	Researched
Coached	Initiated	Resolved
Collaborated	Inspected	Review
Collected	Instituted	Reviewed
Compiled	Integrated	Revitalised
Conceptualized	Interpreted	Scheduled
Consolidated	Interviewed	Shaped
Consulted	Introduced	Solved
Contracted	Invented	Spearheaded
Convinced	Investigated	Spoke
Coordinated	Lectured	Strengthened
Corresponded	Led	Summarised
Counselled	Listened	Supervised
Created	Litigated	Systematised
Critiqued	Maintained	Taught
Customised	Marketed	Trained
Delegated	Mediated	Translated
Demonstrated	Moderated	Upgrades
Designed	Motivated	Wrote
Developed	Negotiated	
Directed	Operated	

Journal Notes

Produce Polished Photographs

The requisition of photographs is so much more than a simple vanity requirement, and I cannot emphasise their importance enough. Not only will your photographs be the recruiter's first impression of you, they will also serve as a visual reminder for the recruiters to refer back to throughout the assessment process, and when making hiring decisions.

By following the simple guidelines that follow, you can be sure that your photos will make a positive and memorable impression.

Requirements

Each airline will have its own specific requirements, and these will be advised when you apply. For reference, though, you can expect the minimum requisition of a head and shoulder shot, generally in the form of a 45 x 35 mm passport photograph. This may also be accompanied by a request for a full length shot, which is subject to varying specifications.

Formal vs Informal

Casual shots, while acceptable for some airlines, carry the risk of appearing sloppy, unprofessional, and inappropriate. As a result, they present a much higher risk of rejection. Business attire, on the other hand, will give the appearance of professionalism, and it is highly unlikely that they will be rejected.

Set the Scene

A solid backdrop will produce a clean and uncluttered appearance. If possible, use a contrasting colour to avoid blending into the surroundings. White or pastel shades usually suit this purpose well.

Work the Angles

Being aware of your most flattering angles and knowing how to use them in front of the camera will make you appear photogenic. Try experimenting with a digital camera. With shots taken from different angles, it will quickly become obvious which angles are the most flattering for you.

Dress the Part

Whatever style of dress you ultimately choose, whether formal or informal, you need to pay attention to:

» Fit:
Wear clothing that fits your body correctly. Clothing that is too short or too long, too big or too small is never a good look.

» Suitability:
Even if you opt for a casual look, your attire needs to be suitable. Too much cleavage, exposed midriffs, and excessively short skirts are not suitable, so don't do it.

» Patterns:
Some patterns, such as stripes, can have a negative impact on your photos. Horizontal stripes have a tendency to overwhelm and make you look wide, while closely spaced stripes can create weird effects.

» Colours:
Colours, such as black, red and white can cause difficulties with digital cameras and should be worn with caution.

Recommended styles:

» Women:
Business attire can be as casual as a reasonable length skirt or tailored trousers combined with a blouse, or cardigan/sweater combination, or as smart as a matching dress and jacket set.

» Gents:
A collared shirt and trouser combination is acceptable, with a jacket or blazer being optionally added to complete the look.

Quick & Dirty Tips

» Classic model pose:
Arrange your body at a 45 degree angle to the camera and turn your head towards the lens. Place one foot in front of the other and place your weight onto the back leg.

» Instant chin tuck:
The most natural and flattering facial shot is achieved when the camera is at or just above eye level. If the lens is lower, you risk showing a double chin.

» Wide awake eyes:
Try looking slightly above the camera to give your eyes a wide open look. This will also reduce the red eye effect.

Quick & Dirty Tip

Combine a black, dark grey, light grey and royal blue suit with a brightly coloured blouse or unique tie to give the outfit a professional, yet unique character which will stand out.

Mind your Accessories

Jewellery should be minimal and conservative. Wear no more than one ring per hand. Avoid cloth or rope bracelets and thumb rings.

Visible tattoos and facial piercings are not acceptable. Tattoos will need to be concealed and piercings removed.

Tend to your Grooming

Photographs tend to exaggerate complexion issues and flatten your features. Use cosmetics to re-enhance your features, cover blemishes and create an overall polished look. Pay particular attention to the following:

» Balance your assets:
Use colour to emphasise your cheeks, lips and eyes, but be sure to experiment beforehand as colours can appear more intense in photos.

Contouring and highlighting is a clever technique that can be used to create depth, balance your face shape, play down flaws, and emphasise assets. Contouring uses a dark shade and is used to recede areas, while highlighting uses a light shade and is used to protrude areas.

» Control shine:
It is important to control the shine, particularly around the t-zone area (nose and forehead), as this will reflect strongly in photos. For minor shine issues, a powder foundation should do the trick. For more problematic skin, an oil absorbing moisturiser or oil balancing gel may be more suitable.

» Counter redness:
Redness will stand out in photos. If the redness is minimal, a standard foundation should suffice. If you suffer from troublesome redness, a more purposeful green coloured concealer or foundation will certainly minimise the impact to a much higher degree. Use these with caution, though, as they are very heavy duty and can give your skin an excessively pale look.

» Conceal blemishes:
Use concealer or foundation to conceal blemishes such as spots, under eye circles and scars.

» Refresh your eyes:
Eye drops will make your eyes glisten, and clear any redness.

Your hair should be neat and well groomed, and outrageous colours or styles should be avoided.. Frizzy or loose ends can appear messy so should be brushed into place and fixed, but be careful not to produce a slicked down appearance.

Note:

Male cabin crew are not normally permitted to have beards so it is recommended that you are cleanly shaven or maintain a closely trimmed style.

Warm your Smile

A warm and sincere smile will complete the look, but creating a beautiful smile on demand is a learned skill which needs to be practiced.

The fake smile, aptly named the 'Pan-Am Smile' because of the flight attendants of Pan-American Airlines, is simply a courtesy smile that will not translate well in your photos. A 'Duchenne Smile', on the other hand, will provide the most beautiful and sincere looking smile, and this is the smile we are looking to achieve.

Here are some tips that will assist you in generating your photo perfect smile.

Produce a natural smile
The most beautiful smiles are the ones that are natural. If you are using a professional photographer, they will be skilled at drawing out your natural smile, but if you are using an unskilled family member, you will need to channel some of your inner happiness. This can be achieved by thinking of a genuine reason to smile, such as recalling a happy memory, looking at a silly picture, or remembering a good joke.

Fake it till you make it
When it is simply impossible to summons a genuine smile, you will need to fake it. Here's some guidelines that will help.

» Time it right:
The secret to producing a relaxed and natural smile is to time it so that you don't have to hold it for too long. Try looking away from the camera, then just before the photograph is taken, face the camera and smile.

» Use your eyes:
Smiling eyes are required to complete the look. To achieve this effect, imagine the camera is someone you really fancy. Raise your eyebrows and cheekbones a little, and slightly squint the corners of your eyes. Notice the amazing transformation this creates.

Pan-Am Smile

Duchenne Smile

Copyright Paul Ekman 2003, "Emotions Revealed," Owl Books, 2007

Surpass the Telephone Screening

In a quest to save time and money, some airlines are now adopting telephone screening techniques. The telephone screening allows selectors to determine a candidate's eligibility, and then eliminate unsuitable candidates without going to the expense of inviting them to attend an interview.

The information you supply at this stage is vital to your continuation in the process so you need to be prepared. Thus, I have devised the following guidelines to give you the best chance of success.

Format

Telephone screenings vary between airlines and, generally, come in two formats:

» Quick and general
This style of screening is usually straightforward and consists of a series of simple questions which seek to identify eligibility. For example: Are you over xx" in height?, Are you over xx years old? Do you have customer service experience?

» Deep and detailed
This format is more comparable to a formal interview and you can expect tougher elimination questions. For example: Why do you want to work for us? Why do you want to be cabin crew? Tell me about your weaknesses?

Be Prepared

As soon as you submit a résumé or application form, you should be prepared to receive a call from a recruiter, at any time. Although you cannot control the timing of these calls, there are some precautions you can take to ensure that you are not caught completely off guard.

Outgoing voice mail
For times when you are unable to take a call, a professional outgoing voice mail message will provide the best impression. For example:

"Hello. You have reached Jane Doe's voice mail. I'm sorry I am unable to take your call at present, but please leave your name, telephone number and a short message, and I'll be sure to return your call as soon as possible".

Mobile telephone usage
Where possible, your first choice of contact should be via a land-line telephone. If a mobile phone is unavoidable, however, make sure it has a clear sound and you maintain a full battery.

Prepare for potential questions
To ensure that you can provide precise answers to the recruiter's questions, you should have your résumé in front of you.

Some questions you might expect in a telephone screening are:

- » Can you tell me about yourself and your work history?
- » Why are you leaving your present job?
- » Why do you want to work for us?
- » What interests you about this job?
- » What skills can you bring to the position?

You should also be ready to provide some specific examples of accomplishments and experiences which showcase your customer service and teamwork skills.

Take notes
Keep a pen and paper on hand so that you can write down brief notes about the call, including the callers name and phone number.

If you are offered to attend a formal interview, make a note of the date and time, the location and phone number, and directions to the venue (if offered).

Keep hydrated
Depending on the length of the conversation, and how nervous you become, a dry mouth and throat can become a hazard. For this reason, I would suggest sipping on a glass of water throughout the telephone call.

Make a Positive Impression

Returning missed calls
Return missed calls promptly and be prepared to interview immediately.

If you reach the recruiter's voice mail, you should leave a message using the following guidelines:

- » Speak slowly and clearly
  It goes without saying that the recipient should hear and understand every word.

Speak Clearly

Make a conscious effort to slow the pace of your speech and enunciate clearly. Speaking too fast, too close to the mouthpiece or mumbling will make you harder to understand.

Use Silence

It is easy to talk too much when you are nervous. A moment of silence, while it might seem awkward to you, lets the recruiter know that you are done.

Read more about communication on page 48

» Avoid filler words
Filler words, such as ums and ahs, sound unprofessional. Avoid their use by preparing your message in advance.

» Introduce yourself
Begin the message by introducing yourself and identifying for who the message is for. Example: "Hello. This is a message from Jane Doe for Carrie Loren"

» Leave a short summary message
A short summary detailing your reason for calling is sufficient, such as: "I received your message regarding the cabin crew selection interview and would be eager to discuss the position with you further"

» Close the message
End the call by stating your availability and telephone number(s). For instance: "You can reach me on 01137 483 948 Monday to Friday between 9 and 5, or on my mobile 07897 786 897 from 5 onwards. I look forward to speaking with you shortly".

Use the recruiter's name
To establish rapport, write down the recruiter's name and use it throughout the conversation.

Dress the part
If you are initiating the call, or if you know to expect one, you should make an effort to dress appropriately. This doesn't necessarily mean full business attire, but it does mean something that will make you feel relaxed, yet alert and businesslike. Slacks or a bathrobe will hardly make you feel professional, and it certainly won't put you in the correct frame of mind for a formal telephone conversation.

Keep an upright posture
To give your voice more energy and projection power, try maintaining a good upright posture.

Pay attention to your tone
Your voice plays a key role in sending the correct messages. If your tone sounds bored and distracted, it won't matter how enthusiastically you phrase your answers because your tone will be the message that sticks with the recruiter. The key is to match the sound of your voice to the words you are using.

To check the level of enthusiasm in your voice, you can practice with a tape recorder.

Ask for clarification

If you are unsure or feel you have misunderstood a question, it is better to request the recruiter to repeat, rephrase or summarise the question than to answer the question incorrectly.

Rather than jump straight in with your question, though, you should consider using a polite introductory phrase, such as:

» I beg your pardon, but I don't quite follow/understand. I wonder if you could rephrase that in a different way?

» Do you think you could repeat the part about ... once again please?

» Pardon me. Would you mind repeating that?

» Sorry, but I'm not sure I'm following you.

» Let's see if I understand/understood you correctly ...

» Do you/Does this mean that...

» Would it be correct to say that...

» So in other words...

Faux Pas Alerts

Leading or controlling

Don't try to lead or control the conversation, this is the recruitment officer's Job. You can, however, ask questions of your own when opportunities arise.

Distractions & Interruptions

Minimise potential distractions by taking the call in a quiet room. If you are caught at an inopportune time, politely ask the caller to hold for a brief moment while you move to a quiet location. You could say "Could you give me a moment to go to a room where we won't be interrupted?"

Alternatively, if the timing is really bad, you can respectfully request an alternative date and time by saying "I do apologise, but is there a time I can reach you later? I'm very interested in the position and want to give you my undivided attention, but I'm afraid that now isn't the best time."

Interrupting the recruiter

Unless absolutely necessary, you should never interrupt the recruiter while they are speaking. Write down any questions or comments you have for later.

Verbal Cues

Although you should never interrupt the recruiter, you shouldn't listen in total silence either. Instead, use verbal feedback cues to indicate that you are listening and that you understand. This will encourage the recruiter to continue.

Some verbal feedback signals include:

» "uh huh"

» "I see."

» "Yes"

» "Ok"

» "I understand"

» "That's interesting"

» "Sure"

» "Right"

» "Of course"

Smile

A smile will add warmth to your voice and make it sound friendly, inviting and enthusiastic. To give yourself a boost, there are several things you can do:

» Keep a humorous, inspirational or special picture nearby

» Keep a mirror in front of you as a reminder to smile

» Think about someone you care about

» Have a funny joke pinned up

» Have some happy music playing in the background (make sure it is appropriate music though and not too loud)

Negativity

There is no room for negativity when it comes to interviews of any kind. Be especially careful when discussing other jobs, airlines, people, previous employers and your current job.

Puff Puff, Slurp Slurp

Any sounds you make close to the receiver will be amplified at the other end so avoid smoking, eating and drinking close to the mouthpiece.

Umm, Anyways

Anyways, you know how when you are, like, really nervous, and you ,ummm, find it hard to verbalise and stuff and you say silly things that, kind of, make you sound, like, kind of, unprofessional and maybe, like, inarticulate?

The useless and annoying verbal mannerisms used in the above example "you know," "like," "in other words," "kind of," "ummm," and "anyways." should be avoided at all costs. Besides making you sound unprofessional, they also detract attention from your message.

Unprepared or unnecessary questions

To stand out as an informed and competent applicant, your questions should reflect that you have researched the airline and the position. Asking questions that have already been addressed within the airline's literature will make you appear unprepared and incompetent.

Likewise, asking questions that are based on money and benefits will make you appear selfishly motivated and give a negative impression about your motives for the position and/or the airline.

Making a Successful Close

As the recruitment officer begins to conclude the interview thank him or her for their time and, if they haven't suggested an in person interview, enquire about the next steps and tell them that you are available for a face-to-face interview.

For example: "I've really enjoyed talking to you and am very interested in the position. What are the next steps in the hiring process? Should I expect to hear from you soon?"

Journal Notes

Concluding Notes

Proofreading Checklist

When proofreading your work, be mindful of:

» Spellings and typos
» Grammar and punctuation
» Factuality
» Sentence structure
» Logic
» Consistency of word usage

Proofread, Proofread, Proofread

The importance of proofreading your documents cannot be emphasised enough. Mistakes in grammar, punctuation and spelling reflect badly on your effort and may be the excuse a selector needs when trying to 'thin the pack'.

With so much importance resting on the final presentation, I have devised a list of guidelines to assist you in proofreading your work:

» Use a spell checker
  The built in spell checker within most word processing programs can help you catch some basic errors such as, repeated words and reversed letters. Don't rely too heavily on these, however, as they are by no means perfect.

» Give it a rest
  If time allows, set aside your work for at least a few hours. When you return, you will have fresh eyes and will be able to spot errors much more efficiently.

» Prepare
  Proofreading requires concentration, patience, and time. Proofread at a time when you are most alert, not rushed and less likely to be distracted.

» Use a checklist
  If there are words that you regularly misspell or misuse, make a note of these and cross reference them each time you proofread.

» Review a hard copy
  Reviewing your work in an alternative format may reveal errors that you may have otherwise missed.

» Break it down
  Rather than carrying out one large proofread, break the process down into smaller, specific proofreads. For instance, use the first pass for spelling, the second for punctuation, the third for grammar, and so on.

» Slowly does it
  Proofread each paragraph one by one, sentence by sentence, word by word.

» Work backwards
  Working backwards through the text is the best way to catch spelling errors as it focuses your mind on the individual words, rather than the context of a complete sentence.

» Use your ears
One of the best ways to edit and proofread your work is to read it out loud. Missing words, lack of clarity, or even phrasing that just doesn't sound quite right, can be picked up better when read aloud.

» Seek assistance
A new set of eyes will certainly spot some errors that you have overlooked, so invite a friend or relative to assist you in the process.

What Happens Next?

Those who are successful at the application stage are usually contacted within six weeks of the application close-off date and invited to attend a preliminary selection process.

In the unfortunate case that you have been unsuccessful, you may or may not receive a rejection letter.

Journal Notes

Part 4

Attend

....

Introduction
Group Activities
Individual Assessments
Panel Interview

Introduction

What to Expect

There is no set formula as to how many or which combination of activities are included during airline assessments, however, the process is typically divided into three key segments, these are: Group activities, individual assessments and a panel interview.

» Group activities
  During the group segment, you will be asked to take part in several activities. These activities are designed to reveal your personality, competencies and potential for working as cabin crew and are likely to include a series of practical tasks, group discussions and role plays.

» Individual assessments
  Individual assessments may be paper based, such as personality questionnaires and general knowledge tests, or they may be practical, such as self presentations, language proficiency and reach tests. Either way, these assessments form an integral part of the eligibility criteria.

» Panel interview
  A typical panel interview will take place before two or three recruitment officers. While each member of the panel will have an opportunity to pose questions to the candidate, it is common practice to have a primary examiner to ask questions and a secondary examiner to observe and take notes.

Attendance
The volume of attendees will depend on the airline and the assessment procedure. Typically, invitation only assessment days will accommodate fewer than 30 candidates, while open days can attract a hundred or more.

Venue
Invitation only assessments and final interviews are typically held at the airlines own premises. Open days attract a larger attendance so will commonly be held within a hotel establishment.

Schedule
The assessment process varies considerably in length and structure depending on a number of factors. In some instances, they may span only a few short hours. In other cases, they may be split over a series of days. Your invitation letter or the airlines website will provide further confirmation of the predicted schedule.

For reference, panel interviews may be as short as 20 minutes or as long as two hours. A typical open day will be a two day event and might run as follows:

Day One
9:00   Arrive, welcome and introductory briefing
9:15   Airline presentation and icebreaker session
10:00   Forms completion and written exercise
10:30   Group session, coffee beak and first eliminations
12:30   Lunch break
1:30   Group session, coffee break and second eliminations
3:00   Individual assessments and mini interview
4:30   Debrief
5:00   Depart

Day Two
9:00   Day Two will typically be filled from 9:00 - 5:00 with blocks
5:00   of panel interviews.

Eliminations
Up until the panel interview, eliminations of unsuccessful candidates will take place periodically throughout the event. Depending on the airline, this will usually take place in groups at specific intervals.

Meet the Candidates

Whether you are attending an invitation only assessment or an open day, you can expect upwards of 20 candidates to be present. As this may be a daunting prospect for some, I have devised some guidelines and strategies that will carry you through and see you shine.

Friend or foe?
Whether fellow candidates are friends or foes matters not. The recruiters will be assessing your ability to positively interact with others so it is important to be friendly, considerate and respectful to everyone you meet.

Successful interaction
Successful interaction comes from understanding and respecting an individuals' personality. Read through the following personality guidelines to learn how to effectively interact with the varying types you are likely to encounter.

» The Aggressor
The aggressors that you will encounter in an interview environment are often covert and manipulative. They disguise their attacks as constructive criticism or harmless jokes so that, in the instance that they are confronted, they can deny any wrong doing. If you find yourself under attack from these predators, ask questions that will temp them into the open, such as: "That sounded like a disrespectful comment, was it?"

If the aggressor is more openly disrespectful and disparaging, the best approach is to remain calm and composed, listen attentively and without interruption until they have finished. A counter attack will only reflect badly on you so resist the tendency to fight back. Instead, acknowledge their opinion and then voice your own in a respectful manner.

» The Extrovert
Extroverts are very sociable creatures and thrive on interaction. They are comfortable speaking to large audiences, are very open with their thoughts and feelings, and take an enthusiastic approach to most activities.

As these extroverted types love to network, any time spent in discussion with them may be somewhat limited. While in their presence, enjoy the buzz they create and allow their enthusiasm to radiate through you.

If you have an introverted tendency, there may be a potential personality clash. Just bide you time and try to enjoy their vibrant presence.

» The Desperado
Some candidates will be in a position of sheer desperation for the job. Whether this is due to a real need or a simple desire, these individuals are likely to appear anxious and tense. Be friendly and empathetic with these candidates, but avoid getting drawn too deeply into conversation about of their hardship.

» The Model
In using the term 'model', I am not necessarily referring to looks. Rather, I am referring to those candidates who seem to be models of perfection. They appear to say and do all the right things, seemingly without a care or worry in the world. They naturally exude charisma and confidence, and have a magnetic personality.

In observing these candidates, examine what makes them appear perfect and then learn by their example. How do they stand? What do they do with their hands? How do they use their voice?

» The Overly Anxious
Some individuals become overwhelmed at interviews and will experience intense levels of stress, fear and panic. In this heightened state, the individual may experience uncontrollable symptoms such as blushing, stammering and shaking.

Experiencing a panic attack is very traumatic, so be friendly and supportive with these individuals. Offer words of encouragement, but don't place too much focus on their anxiety. Rather, try to break their state by asking questions about things they enjoy and that make them feel relaxed. You could ask them about their family, hobbies or desires.

» The Dominator
Can't get a word in? You may be encountering the dominator. In milder cases, dominators like to be the centre of attention and will talk incessantly to control the conversation. In extreme cases, they will be argumentative, rude and irrational.

In the face of a domineering person, remain calm and resist the natural urge to reason or retaliate. Instead, you should either try to distance yourself from the person, otherwise an assertive communication style is needed to push past this stickler. In this instance, remain calm, confident and respectful.

» The Actor
Actors in this context refers to those candidates who put on an elaborate front to conceal their true personalities. These individuals are usually relatively harmless so, if you do happen to catch their act, it is probably best to not blow their cover.

If, however, it becomes obvious that this candidate has blatantly lied for the job, you may want to distance yourself to avoid being associated with their deceit.

» The Know-It-All
Know-it-alls have an attitude of superiority and like to think they are experts in everything. In conversation, they are arrogant and condescending and openly disregard the opinion of others. Some know-it-alls really are experts, so just agree with them and try to move on. If, however, the so called expert is not an expert at all, simply state the facts as you perceive them. Whatever you do, don't be drawn into a debate with either type because it will get messy.

» The Negativist
Ah, the negativist. There's always one in every crowd. At best, negativists are very annoying. At worst, they will drain every ounce of energy and motivation from your body. Attempts to motivate or encourage these people generally fall flat, so it's sometimes best not to say anything at all. So, remain positive and try to distance yourself as much as possible. If this is not possible, detach yourself from their words and stay focused on your own positive energy.

» The Leader
Natural leaders are instantly recognisable by their innate desire to step up. Their confident, assertive and intelligent character inspires trust in others while their sensitive, inspiring and sincere side inspires confidence. In the presence of a good leader, respect, support and encourage their efforts. Participate and be an active member of their team.

» The Show-off
You can be certain to find a show-off at every cabin crew interview. You will recognise him or her by their showy, self absorbed and obnoxious attitude. While this personality type is easily annoying, the truth is that these people tend to be deeply insecure. They brag about their own achievements through fear that nobody will otherwise notice. So, be kind and sincerely acknowledge their efforts when appropriate.

» The Rival
Naturally there will be candidates present who view you as competition and a threat to their success. Being competitive isn't a bad thing in itself unless these candidates put up barriers and become inwardly focused. In this instance, it is important to be friendly while respectful of their space. Remember, competitive people are passionate, driven and innovative, so embrace these positive traits.

» The Gossiper
Some individuals like to point out other peoples flaws or failures in an attempt to feel superior. Beware of these gossiping individuals as you can be sure they will gossip about you too. In the first instance, attempt to change the subject. If they continue, discourage their behaviour directly by refusing to participate. If all fails, take your leave immediately.

» The Entertainer
Entertainers thrive on interaction. They are sociable, talkative and very energetic people and love to be the centre of attention. It is very easy to like the entertainer as they have a very down to earth and friendly attitude. When interacting with an entertainer, avoid being overly serious and just allow their positive energy to flow through you.

Meet the Recruitment Officers

Typically, there will be two or three official recruitment officers present during recruitment days. These officers may be HR personnel, or they may be working senior crew members. Either way, you can be sure that they are experienced recruitment professionals.

Successful interaction

To successfully interact with recruitment personnel, it is important to understand their styles and be prepared to deal with them accordingly. Within a cabin crew interview setting, you will typically encounter two dominant styles of interviewer. I call these: The interrogation experts and the guardian angels.

» The interrogation expert
Interrogation experts believe that candidates will only show their true personalities while under intense pressure. As a result, they adopt a direct and intimidating style of questioning and will cross examine every answer you provide. During this onslaught of questioning, they will be observing your ability to remain calm and think on your feet. So, approach their questions in a calm and confident manner and be direct and succinct in your response.

» The guardian angel
Guardian angels believe that candidates are more open and natural when they feel relaxed. Thus, they will attempt to relieve the pressure of the atmosphere by engaging in friendly conversation. While their relaxed and friendly style can be a welcome relief, unsuspecting candidates may become overly casual and reveal more than is appropriate. Thus, caution is advised. The key is to be friendly yet professional, and never let your guard down.

Meet the Undercover Team

To help the recruitment officers make informed decisions and better elimination choices, undercover officers are often placed among the group during recruitment days. Within the role of a fellow candidate, these officers can observe individuals in their relaxed and natural state and be in a better position to identify unsuitable candidates.

These officers are largely accountable for the high percentage of failure rates that candidates experience during the group stage. They are also the reason why some candidates leave the interview feeling confused about their elimination.

Unfortunately, these officers are very good at their jobs, so there is little chance that you will ever identify them. However, simply being aware of their presence will give you a great advantage as you will be able to adapt your strategy to avoid this devastating outcome.

Impress

To impress undercover officers, you simply need to treat everyone you meet in the same positive manner. If you are friendly, respectful and supportive towards your fellow candidates, have a positive outlook and are able to demonstrate an enthusiastic attitude towards any activities which you are asked to undertake, the officers will naturally pick up on your positive energy.

The tests

To really get to the bare bones of a candidates personality, some undercover officers will conduct a series of mini personality tests. During these tests, the officer will demonstrate certain traits and then observe your reactions to them. For instance: Do you actively participate in mindless gossip, or do you show disapproval? Are you sympathetic and encouraging towards anxious candidates, or are you unsupportive and dismissive? Are you constructive in your criticism, or do you attack others ideas?

As long as you discourage others bad behaviour and actively demonstrate a positive attitude, these tests will not pose any threat to your success. In the worst instance, remain neutral until you can safely distance yourself.

Group Activities

What Assessors Look For

Through your involvement and behaviour, assessors will be looking for evidence of key competencies and personality attributes that will enable you to work effectively as cabin crew and cope with the demands of the job.

The six key competencies that will be assessed are:

» Communication skills   » Team spirit

» Interpersonal ability   » Leadership

» Customer focus   » Initiative

To determine these competencies, the assessors will be observing:

» Level of participation and interaction

» Behaviour towards the activities and your peers

» Communication and work style

» Ability to think on your feet and react to external pressure

» Ability to lead and willingness to follow

To make an effective evaluation, the recruiters will typically refer to a competency rating scale. This scale works on a points based system and the final result will reflect a candidates suitability for the position.

Competency Rating Scale

-1 Unacceptable	0 Needs Improvement	1 Effective	2 Proficient	3 Outstanding

3	Works effectively as a team member and builds strong relationships within it
0	Remains calm and confident, and responds logically and decisively in difficult situations
3	Understands other people's views and takes them into account
2	Contributes ideas and collaborates with the team
2	Takes a systematic approach to problem solving
3	Speaks with authority and confidence
3	Is thoughtful and tactful when dealing with people
-1	Is conscientious of completing tasks on time
3	Actively supports and encourages others
2	Participates as an active and contributing member of the team

Figure 11.   Competency Rating Scale Sample Form

Seven Heavenly Virtues

1. Have fun
   However silly or irrelevant the tasks may seem, your active involvement is essential. So, rather than concern yourself about external details, just relax and allow yourself to enjoy the process. This positive viewpoint will reflect well on your character, demonstrate enthusiasm, and make the experience a fun filled one for you.

2. Contribute
   Volunteering, contributing ideas and making suggestions is another great way to demonstrate your enthusiasm and team spirit. Furthermore, it will show that you are not afraid to take the initiative or express yourself and are keen to get involved.

3. Keep track of time
   If the recruiters set a time limit for any task, it is respectful to honour the deadline. Moreover, it will reflect positively on your listening skills, and demonstrate your attention to detail and ability to follow instructions. So, remain vigilant of the time and forewarn your peers when the deadline is approaching.

4. Summarise
   Summarising the main points of a discussion is a great way to move past awkward moments of silence and sticking points. The breathing room summarising creates will typically stimulate further ideas and encourage participation. Not only will your peers be grateful for the momentary relief, your communication and leadership ability will also be highlighted.

5. Use names
   Remembering people's names will demonstrate your ability to listen and pay attention to detail. Moreover, it will demonstrate a tremendous amount of respect for others and create a lasting impact.

6. Be positive
   When you choose to exhibit a positive spirit, people will naturally be drawn towards your character. So, be enthusiastic about the exercises you are asked to undertake and be encouraging towards others.

7. Encourage
   If any members of your team remain reserved, encourage their involvement by asking if they have an idea, suggestion or opinion. This shows empathy, consideration team spirit.

Seven Deadly Sins

1. Over involvement
   Getting involved and showing enthusiasm in a task is fantastic, but over involvement and incessant talking can leave others struggling to get involved and may transfer across to assessors as arrogance.

2. Under involvement
   For assessors to make an informed assessment, active involvement from each individual is essential. Those who are unable to get involved, for whatever reason, will surely be eliminated.

3. Disputing
   Conflicting views are natural, however, a group assessment is neither the time or place to engage in a hostile dispute with other candidates.

4. Criticising
   Even if your intentions are honourable and the feedback is constructive, criticising another candidates opinions, actions and ideas may be perceived as an attack.

5. Being negative
   Making negative remarks or exhibiting frustration over tasks, peers or previous employers , no matter how harmless it may seem, will raise serious concerns about your attitude and ethics.

6. Being bossy
   There is nothing wrong with striving for excellence, however, being dominant and imposing your ideas on others is overbearing and intimidating which leads others to feel incompetent.

7. Neglecting to listen
   Neglecting to listen to instructions leads to misinterpretations and displays a general lack of enthusiasm. Not listening or talking over others is ignorant and disrespectful.

Common Concerns

Being alienated

When there are a lot of different personalities in a group and the emotions are high, it can become difficult to get involved. This is especially true during a large group discussion. In these instances, you should employ some of the following strategies for getting your voice heard.

» Raise your hand
As simple as it seems, raising your hand will demand the attention of the group and let them know that you have something to say.

» Be assertive
If raising your hand reaps no results, you will have to be more assertive. Wait for a momentary pause in the conversation, and simple say "excuse me" before proceeding. This may feel uncomfortable for some of you, but it is imperative that you contribute. If done calmly and respectfully, the assessors will be impressed by your effort.

Dealing with anxiety

If you have read through and practised the techniques described on pages 31 through 45, you should not experience much difficulty in dealing with symptoms of anxiety.

For on the spot relief, the most effective techniques are:

» Subtle deep breathing (Page 41)

» Trigger positive anchors (Page 34)

» Silently repeat affirmations (Page 39)

» Change your focus (Page 39)

Whichever technique you use, don't allow it to distract your attention too much that you lose the flow of the discussion or task.

Handling disagreements

If you disagree with an approach being taken by the group or an idea which has been brought forth, it is perfectly reasonable to say so as long as you are constructive and positive in doing so.

Consider the following statements:

» Negative:
"That wouldn't work. I think we should…"

» Constructive:
"I see your point, Mark, but there are a number of issues that may arise with that approach. How about we consider…"

The former example attacks and ridicules the idea, while the latter demonstrates a positive acknowledgement before a new idea is introduced.

In the instance that your new idea is rejected, remain polite and seek input from the group. If you are clearly outnumbered, gracefully accept the decision and move on.

Being ridiculed
If your idea is ridiculed, resist the temptation to retaliate. Instead, remain cordial and respectful in your response. This graceful reaction will be duly noted and respected by the assessors.

Feeling uncertain
You don't always have to give an opinion when you speak. Supporting what someone else has said, asking a legitimate question, or commenting on an emerging theme are equally good ways to make your presence known without appearing as if you like the sound of your own voice.

Points to Consider

In most cases, the outcome of each task or topic is largely irrelevant. Assessors are more concerned with how well you perform in a team environment, how you communicate your ideas and interact with others, and what role you typically assume.

Thus, no matter how you feel, you should approach every task with a can do attitude and every topic in a calm and conversational tone.

Journal Notes

Practical Tasks

Bridging the Gap
Advertising Space
Let me Entertain You
Attention Please
Who's Who?
Designer Wear

Bridging the Gap

Duration: 30 Minutes

Instructions

With the materials provided, design and construct a bridge which strong enough to support a roll of sticky tape.

Materials

- » 5 sheets of A4 paper
- » A pair of scissors
- » 1 Metre length of sticky tape
- » 4 Drinking straws
- » 1 Metre length of string
- » 2 Elastic bands

Advertising Space

Duration: 40 Minutes

Instructions

Fly High Airlines has secured a prime time radio spot and needs a new commercial campaign.

Using the teams collective knowledge of the airline, create a compelling commercial that will attract new customers.

The final broadcast must be no more than 45 seconds in length, and each team member must have an active role in the final presentation.

Points to Consider

This activity will highlight your knowledge of the airline, so be ready with plenty of input from your research.

Let Me Entertain You Duration: 40 Minutes

Instructions

As you reach cruising altitude, you discover that the in flight entertainment system has failed. To ensure the passengers are entertained for the duration of the four hour flight, design a game concept and present it to the rest of the group in a teaching style.

Attention Please   Duration: 45 Minutes

Instructions

Many passengers ignore safety demonstrations because they feel they have heard it all before.

In an effort to increase safety, Fly High Airlines is considering an overhaul of its safety procedures.

As a group, come up with a safety demonstration which will encourage passengers to pay attention to these important briefings.

The demonstration can include appropriate humour, choreography and melodies, but the outcome should be no more than five minutes in length.

Who's Who?

Duration: 20 Minutes

Instructions

Pair off with a random partner and try to find out as much as you can about each other in twenty minutes.

When called upon, present your partner to the group.

Points to Consider

The purpose of this task is threefold.:

» How relevant is the information you gather?

» How confident are you when addressing a group?

» How well do you interact with new people.

Designer Wear

Duration: 45 Minutes

Instructions

Fly High Airlines is looking to update its image and needs new designs for its cabin crew uniform.

Consider the existing design and come up with a new or modified concept.

Points to Consider

During this task, be mindful of what is considered appropriate to the culture.

Also, take inspiration from the current design as it provides valuable insight into what the airline considers to be appropriate.

Discussions

Shipwrecked
Survivor
Rags to Riches
Day Trip

Shipwrecked

Duration: 45 Minutes

Instructions

The plane has gone down over the Atlantic Ocean. There are eight survivors, but the one surviving life raft only has a capacity for four people.

As a team, identify four survivors from the following list who you would save and why. Select a spokesperson to present your decision and explain why you came up with the results.

Survivors

- » The pilot
- » A pregnant woman
- » An ex army general
- » A surgeon
- » The pope
- » A child
- » A nurse
- » An athlete

Points to Consider

Due to the very nature of this task, there is a potential for some strong emotions to be released. In such instances, remain calm and don't be tempted into a confrontation. Simply acknowledge and show respect for others opinions.

Survivor

Duration: 45 Minutes

Instructions

Your flight is scheduled to land in Los Angeles, however, due to mechanical difficulties the plane was forced to land on a remote island.

During landing, much of the equipment aboard was damaged, but 10 items have been recovered intact. Your task is to rank them in terms of their importance for your crew.

Items

» A box of matches

» 15 feet of nylon rope

» 5 gallons of water

» Signal flares

» A self inflating life raft

» A magnetic compass

» First aid kit

» A fruit basket

» A tub of dry milk powder

» A shotgun

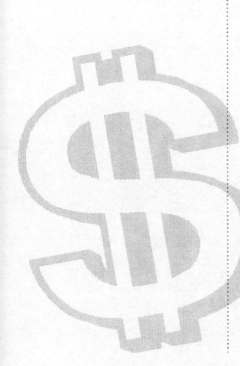

Rags to Riches

Duration: 30 Minutes

Instructions

You have just won £1,000,000.00 on the lottery. From the five options below, which action would you take and why?

Options

» Take early retirement

» Give a large percentage to charity

» Invest it into a business

» Save it for your future

» Spend it on luxuries

Day Trip

Duration: 30 Minutes

Instructions

You have been given the responsibility for arranging a day trip for 15 disabled children. Discuss where you would take the children, what activities you would have arranged and why.

Options

- » Theme park
- » Museum
- » White water rafting
- » Trip on the Orient Express
- » Water Park
- » Safari
- » Art gallery
- » Scenic helicopter ride

Points to Consider

In this instance, the children in question are disabled. So, certain activities will not be appropriate, while others may not sufficiently capture the children's interest. It is important to gain a balance between having fun and being safe.

Role Play Scenarios

Role play scenarios may be performed with other candidates as a pair or within a group, or they may be performed one on one with an assessor.

The scenarios will bear some relation to the demands of the job and are likely to include:

» Intoxicated passenger	» Toilet smoker
» Disorderly behaviour	» Abusive behaviour
» Terrorist threat	» Fearful passenger
» Disruptive child	» Passenger complaint

The assessors don't expect you to know the answer to every possible scenario they introduce. They simply want to see how you react in challenging situations. So, when taking part in any role play scenario, use the following guidelines:

» Be proactive and do your best to resolve the situation using your initiative

» Remain calm and composed

» Be direct and assertive

» Immerse yourself into the role

» Take each scenario seriously

» Devise a plan and follow it as much as possible

Here are some pointers to help you deal with some common scenarios:

» Complaint
   In the case of a passenger complaint, it is important that you listen to their concern without interruption. Ask questions, where appropriate, to clarify their concerns and show empathy towards their situation. If the facts warrant it, apologise for the situation, explain what action you intend to take and thank them for bringing the matter to your attention.

» Fearful passenger
If a passenger is fearful of flying, be considerate of their feelings. Use a gentle and calm tone to talk them through the flight and reassure them of any sounds or sensations they may experience. Let the passenger know where you can be found and show them the call bell.

» Intoxicated passenger
Offer the passenger a cup of tea or coffee and don't provide any more alcoholic drinks. You could also encourage the passenger to eat some food. Remain calm towards the passenger, but be direct and assertive in your approach. If you feel it appropriate, inform your senior and seek assistance from other crew members.

Individual Assessments

Self Introduction

As well as learning more about you and your background, the self introduction is an opportunity for the recruiters to assess how well you cope when addressing a group of people and how articulately you are able to communicate your message. In their assessment, they will be looking for good delivery, and a certain amount of charisma.

To deliver a self introduction which makes an impact, here are some guidelines for you to consider.

» Make it relevant
Use this opportunity to highlight your suitability for the job of cabin crew by sharing interesting facts about your present or most recent job, and your motives for making a career change.

Consider the following example:
" Hi everyone. My name is Jane and it's really nice to meet you all. I'm 27 years old and live in the bustling city of Bristol. I currently work as a freelance hair consultant, which is a job I really enjoy, but I have always wanted to be cabin crew which is why I am here today. Outside of work, I enjoy horse riding and am captain of the local football team"

» Be spontaneous
A self presentation which is spontaneous will add life and sincerity to your speech. Sure you can prepare a rough draft and familiarise yourself with it, but don't try to learn it by heart as there is a risk of appearing forced, dull and monotone.

» Inject personality
Show your passion and enthusiasm by injecting some emotion into your presentation.

» Be concise
Unless advised otherwise, keep it relatively short and focused. Thirty to Sixty seconds should be sufficient.

» Rotate your focus
To give the impression of confidence and engage your audience, rotate your gaze and make eye contact with various members for three to five seconds each.

» Adjust your voice
Varying your tone, pitch, volume and pace will eliminate monotone and make it enjoyable for others to listen to. Slowing your pace slightly will also add clarity.

» Stick to the time limit
If a time limit has been set, be sure to respect it.

Personality Questionnaire

Through a series of simple questions, personality tests provide assessors with an indication of a candidates character, behaviour and work style. The test results merely supplement the recruiters own observations from the interview and, as such, there are no right or wrong answers.

Typical questions you will encounter are:

For each question, give a mark out of five. One = Disagree strongly | Five = Agree strongly
» I enjoy meeting new people.
» I get bored with repetitive tasks.
» I often lose my temper when I am frustrated.
» I always think before I act.
» I work well under pressure.
» I find it easy to relax.
» I get on well with most people.
» I am a team player.
» I prefer to work alone.
» I become nervous in social situations.
» I find it difficult to communicate with other cultures.
» I thrive on challenges.

In an attempt to create a favourable impression, some candidates try to imagine how the recruiters want them to be and will answer questions dishonestly. I would advise against this strategy because any contradiction between your answers and the recruiters own observations will make it obvious that the answers have been embellished.

Language Proficiency Test

If a second language is a requirement of the airline or if English isn't your native language, you may be required to complete a language assessment based on the following four key skills:

» Listening

» Reading

» Writing

» Speaking

Tips for Success

When completing any kind of written test, it is important that you read the questions through fully and make sure you completely understand what is being asked before attempting to answer.

To be confident that you have answered as many questions as possible, it is always best to complete the questions you find easy on the first pass, returning to the trickier questions later.

To avoid handing in a form that is full of scribbles and mistakes, mark your answers out in pencil and carry out a final proof-read before you hand in your form.

Performance will be evaluated by how well the candidate understands and can be understood.

Listening

In this section of the test, you will have the chance to show how well you understand the spoken language.

Questions you may come across are as follows:

» You will see a picture, and you will hear four short statements. When you hear the statements, look at the picture and choose the statement that best describes what you see in the picture.

» You will hear a question or statement, followed by three responses. You are to choose the best response to each question or statement.

» You will hear a short conversation between two people. You will then read a question about each conversation. The question will be followed by four answers. You are to choose the best answer to each question.

Reading

In this section of the test, you will have the chance to show how well you understand the written language.

Here are some examples:

Choose one word which best completes the following sentence.

Because the equipment is very delicate, it must be handled with _____.

(A) Caring   (B) Careful   (C) Care   (D) Carefully

Identify one underlined word which should be corrected or rewritten.

All <u>employees</u> are <u>repaired</u> to <u>wear</u> their <u>identification</u> badges while at work.

(A) employees   (B) repaired   (C) wear   (D) identification

Writing & Speaking

In the written and spoken sections of the test, you will have the chance to show how well you speak and write the language.

You may be asked basic questions about your home town, family, work or study, leisure and future plans.

Numerical Ability Test

Numeracy tests are designed to test your basic arithmetic skills: Addition, subtraction, multiplication and division. While they are typically short and relatively simple in nature, if you haven't exercised your maths brain for some time, it may be a good idea to practice some basic mental arithmetic before the interview.

Here are some sample questions to get your juices flowing.

Calculators may or may not be permitted.

1. What is Twelve Thousand Nine Hundred and Seventy Six in figures?
A. 129,76.00   B. 12,976,000   C. 12,976.00

2. What is 6 multiplied by 8?
A. 48   B. 52   C. 46

3. Add 67 to 12
A. 80   B. 79   C. 76

4. You begin with a float of 66.94. A customer purchases a pack of peanuts at 0.66, a shot of spirits at 3.54 and a pack of chewing gum at 0.53. How much float should you have following this transaction?
A. 62.21   B. 71.76   C. 71.67

5. There are 357 seats on your aircraft. The seats are divided into three cabins. How many seats are in each cabin?
A. 117   B. 119   C. 109

Medical Questionnaire

The preemployment medical questionnaire is a simple form which asks you to confirm your current level of medical health and declare any history of serious illness, or drug and alcohol abuse.

Affirming certain conditions isn't an automatic failure of your application, so complete the form as accurately as possible. If you have had a condition which has been treated or is being successfully controlled, clearly state this.

Don't lie or leave out important information as it will be evident when the full medical examination is carried out by the airline.

Tips for Success

» Run through your times tables
» Practice some basic calculations like subtraction and multiplication
» Practice estimating answers without the use of a calculator
» Read each question and answer carefully - sometimes multiple choice answers are deliberately similar so take time to check each option. Pay particular attention to things like the unit of measurement or the number of decimal places.

Reach Test

Where an airline doesn't have a minimum height requirement, they may have a reach requirement instead. A reach requirement simply requires the ability to reach necessary components inside the aircraft which are typically between 6' (182 cm) and 6'10" (212 cm).

To determine candidates reach ability, a simple reach test may be conducted whereby a mark is placed on the wall, typically 6'10" from the floor, and the candidate is asked to reach for the line from their bare feet.

Fly High Airlines

Preemployment Medical Questionnaire

Please ensure all sections of this form are completed. Failure to do so will cause delays

Confidential

Declaration

I can verify that I am not aware of any medical condition that would prohibit my completion of the physical aspects of the training program or ongoing employment as a cabin crew member.

I hereby declare that the answers to the questions within this form are correct to the best of my knowledge and belief, and that I have not withheld any relevant information or made any misleading statements. I understand that incorrect answers may prejudice my employment with Fly High Airlines.

I am aware that further action may be required to investigate a medical condition, and that additional information will be provided to me in relation to this at a later date, if applicable.

Date: 29/01/11   Signature: Printed Name: JANE DOE

Present Address	**Permanent Address** *(If different)*
22 ANY STREET ANY TOWN ANY WHERE	N/A
Post Code AN2 6DG Country U.K	Post Code N/A Country N/A

Please give telephone numbers in the format: Country Code + City/Mobile Code + Phone Number

Telephone (Residence)	44 1179 637264	Telephone (Residence)	N/A
Telephone (Mobile)	44 798 837472	Telephone (Mobile)	N/A
Email	JANE.DOE@ANYMAIL.COM		

Position Sought:	CABIN CREW	Gender:	FEMALE
Date of Birth:	11/09/1979	Hair Colour:	BROWN
Height (cm) 154	Weight (kg) 49	Eye Colour:	BROWN

Your Health Practitioner

Name:	DR SUSAN ANDREWS		
Address:	ANY MEDICAL CENTRE ANY WHERE	*Please give telephone numbers in the format: Country Code + City/Mobile Code + Phone Number*	
		Telephone:	44 1176 677232
Post Code:	AN8 7SB	Fax:	44 1176 677239
Country:	UNITED KINGDOM	Email:	S.ANDREWS@ANYMEDICAL.COM

Figure 12.   Sample Preemployment Medical Form - Page 1

Please continue your answers to the following questions on a separate sheet if necessary.

Have you ever been rejected or discharged from any form of employment for medical reasons? If 'yes' state where, when and why. ➡ NO

Have you lost time from work in excess of one week on account of illness or injury? If 'yes' state approximate dates, time lost and reasons. ➡ I CAME DOWN WITH FLU DURING 2007 AND HAD TO TAKE 9 DAYS LEAVE.

How much time have you had off work due to illness in the last 2 years? State number of occasions and reasons. ➡ 9 DAYS LEAVE FOR FLU DURING 2007

Have you ever received disability payments? (including National Health Benefits) If 'yes' give details. ➡ NO

Have you ever received compensation for any illness or injury sustained at work? If 'yes' give details. ➡ NO

Have you ever been a patient in a hospital, nursing home, clinic, mental hospital or institution? If 'yes' where, when and why. ➡ NO

Are you suffering from any physical illness or disease at this time? If 'yes' give details. ➡ NO

Are you taking or do you routinely take any drugs or medications? If 'yes' give details (this includes contraceptive pill if applicable). ➡ I TAKE THE DEPO PROVERA CONTRACEPTIVE PILL QUARTERLY SINCE 2005

Do you drink alcohol? If 'yes' what is your average weekly intake in units? ➡ NO

Do you smoke? If 'yes' in what form and quantity. ➡ NO

Do you, or have you ever had alcohol, drug or substance abuse? If 'yes' please give details. ➡ NO

Do you or have you ever suffered with gynaecology/menstrual/abdominal/pelvic problems? If 'yes' please give details. ➡ NO

Please continue your answers to the following questions on a separate sheet if necessary.

Figure 13.   Sample Preemployment Medical Form - Page 2

Are you suffering or have you suffered from any condition that the airline should be made aware of? If 'yes' please give details. → NO

Has your weight changed by more than 5kg (12lb) in the last 12 months? If 'yes' give details. → NO

Do you suffer or have you suffered from any back problems? → NO

As part of your contract of employment it will be necessary for you to maintain a yellow fever immunisation. Please advise us if and when you have received this. → 1994

Do you have hearing difficulties? If 'yes' please give details. → NO

Do you have normal eyesight with/without glasses/contact lenses? → YES

Have you ever resided or otherwise associated with any person suffering from tuberculosis? If 'yes' state where and when. → NO

Have you any family history of high blood pressure, heart disease, hypertension, diabetes, or cancer? If 'yes' please give details. → MY MOTHER HAS TYPE 2 DIABETES

Have you ever experienced any symptoms of deafness or ear discomfort after air travel? → NO

Have you ever suffered from thrombosis or blood clots in the leg, or other blood disorders? → NO

Allergies

	Yes/No	Severity of reactions
Drugs	NO	
Antibiotics	NO	
Bites	NO	
Stings	NO	
Nuts	NO	
Other (Please Specify)	NO	

Figure 14.   Sample Preemployment Medical Form - Page 3

Please continue your answers to the following questions on a separate sheet if necessary.

Do you suffer from or have a history of:

	Yes/No	If yes, give details
Nervous breakdown or mental illness?	NO	
Frequent headaches or migraine?	NO	
Head injury or concussion?	NO	
Fits, convulsions or epilepsy?	NO	
Tuberculosis?	NO	
Pneumonia, bronchitis or other lung problems?	NO	
Asthma?	NO	
Hayfever or other allergy?	NO	
Heart/vascular conditions?	NO	
Chest pain?	NO	
Undue shortness of breath?	NO	
Swelling of ankles?	NO	
High/low blood pressure?	NO	
Fainting attacks/dizziness or unconsciousness?	NO	
Rheumatic fever?	NO	
Stomach pain or chronic indigestion?	NO	
Peptic ulcer or abdominal pain?	NO	
Bowel trouble?	NO	
Kidney or bladder disease?	NO	
Passing blood in urine or motions?	NO	
Diabetes or endocrine disorder?	NO	
Frequent colds/sinus trouble/nose or throat disorders?	NO	
Earache or ear discharge?	NO	
Skin disease (e.g. eczema, psoriasis etc)?	NO	
Motion sickness?	NO	
Muscle or joint pain?	NO	
Surgical operations or injuries?	NO	

Figure 15.   Sample Preemployment Medical Form - Page 4

General Knowledge Quiz

General knowledge tests are fairly straightforward. The questions cover a broad range of topics and are likely to include political, geographical, historical, entertainment and scientific areas.

Here are some sample test questions to give you a better idea of what to expect.

» In relation to time, what does the abbreviation GMT stand for?

» How many continents are there?

» What is the name of the highest mountain in the world?

» Which is the largest continent?

» What is the capital of the USA?

» In which country would you find the river Nile?

» In which continent would you find Russia?

» Who is the president of the United States?

» Where will the next Olympics be held?

Journal Notes

Panel Interview

What Assessors Look For

Having assessed your involvement during the group session, the recruiters will now seek to explore your motives for applying to their airline and your desire for pursuing a career as cabin crew. Moreover, they will seek to gather information about your work history, character and work ethic to determine whether you will fit the job and airline.

During the interview, they will examine your ability to listen actively, express yourself articulately, confidently and professionally, and answer questions logically and concisely. They will also be paying special attention to how you present yourself.

The Process

To ease you into the interview process and make you feel more open and relaxed, the recruiters will typically open the session with questions about you and your background.

They will then seek to explore your motivation for applying to the airline and making a career change. Questions such as "Why do you want to work for us?" and "Why do you want to be cabin crew?" are common at this stage.

With the interview thoroughly under way, the recruiters will want to determine whether you possess the skills and experience necessary for the position. Here you can expect more probing situational and behavioural questions, such as "When have you provided good customer service?" and "Describe a time when you failed to communicate effectively".

Duration
There appears to be no typical duration for panel interviews. Some of you will be in and out in as little as 20 minutes, while others may find the interview lasts for up to two hours.

Seven Heavenly Virtues

1. Stay focused
   If you fail to control your internal dialogue you will not only lose your composure, but you also risk misunderstanding the question. Remain completely focused on what the recruiter is saying and focus on giving the best possible answer. Concerns about how you look and the outcome should be postponed until after the interview.

2. Listen actively
   Although you should never interrupt the recruiter, you shouldn't listen in total silence either. Instead, use verbal feedback cues to indicate that you are listening and that you understand. This will encourage the recruiter to continue.

   Some verbal feedback signals include: "I see", "Yes", "I understand", "Sure".

3. Inject personality
   Injecting passion and personality into your answers will add life and sincerity. It will also keep the recruiters interested in what you are saying.

4. Be concise
   If an answer is too long-winded, the recruiter will become complacent. Keeping your answers short and concise will retain their attention.

5. Be positive
   A positive spirit will reflect well on your character and allow the recruiters to warm towards you. So, be enthusiastic about the interview and the job, and speak respectfully about your previous employers and positions.

6. Vary your voice
   Varying your tone, pitch, volume and pace will eliminate monotone and make it enjoyable for the recruiters to listen to. Slowing your pace slightly will also add clarity.

7. Maintain eye contact
   Regular, strong eye contact will give the impression of someone who is honest and confident.

   Where there is more than one recruitment officer, you should maintain eye contact with the person who asks you the question while occasionally engaging eye contact with the second recruiter .

Seven Deadly Sins

1. Controlling
   Trying to lead or control the conversation will appear arrogant and disrespectful. Ask questions when appropriate opportunities arise, but allow the recruiter to do his or her job.

2. Interrupting
   Interruptions are rude and disrespectful to the speaker. So, unless absolutely necessary, you should allow the recruiter to finish speaking before responding or asking for clarification.

3. Lying
   If you lie, there will be a very good chance that you will be caught out when the recruiters probe into your answers with follow up questions. If this happens, you could end up looking rather silly and, worse still, any chance of being offered the job will be ruined.

4. Being negative
   Making negative remarks or exhibiting frustration over tasks, peers, other airlines or previous employers, no matter how harmless it may seem, will raise serious concerns about your attitude and ethics.

5. Unprepared or unnecessary questions
   To stand out as an informed and competent applicant, your questions should reflect that you have researched the airline and the position. Asking questions that have already been addressed within the airline's literature will make you appear unprepared and incompetent.

   Likewise, asking questions that are based on money and benefits will make you appear selfishly motivated and give a negative impression about your motives for the position and/or the airline.

6. Talking incessantly
   It's easy to talk too much when nervous, however, it is important to remember that interviews are two-way exchanges. A moment of silence, while it might seem awkward to you, lets the recruiter know that you are done and allows them to move the interview along.

7. Overusing filler words
   The useless and annoying verbal mannerisms "you know," "like," "in other words," "kind of," "ummm," and "anyways." should be avoided at all costs. Besides making you sound unprofessional, they also detract attention from your message.

Journal Notes

Journal Notes

Part 5

Q&A
Survival Guide

....

Competency Questions
Traditional Questions
Interviewing the Interviewer

Competency

Introduction

The theory behind competency-based interview questions (also known as behavioural or situational questions) lies in the belief that how you have behaved and applied certain skills in the past will determine how you will behave in the future. Thus, recruiters use this style of questioning to predict applicants' future performance as well as to determine whether an applicant possesses the particular qualities, skills and experiences required for the job.

Preparing Examples

The key to preparing for competency-based questions is to study the job description and person specification. With this information, you can identify the core competencies that are required and prepare examples that demonstrate those competencies.

Airlines recruiting for cabin crew positions will certainly be looking for candidates who demonstrate:

- » Communication competence
- » Interpersonal ability
- » Customer focus
- » Team spirit
- » Leadership
- » Initiative

When preparing your examples, don't overlook those of a difficult or negative nature as you will surely be asked to illustrate some of these. To say that you haven't faced any difficulties would sound dishonest and naive.

Before you plunge in, however, you need to be very selective in your choices. For instance, it would be unwise to volunteer a negative example that involves a core skill, or one which had an undesirable impact on the company, colleagues or customers.

The most effective answer in this instance is one that shows that you understand that mistakes are occasionally part of the professional growth process, and that you are able to remain calm and learn from these experiences.

The S.A.R.R Formula

S.A.R.R is an acronym for Situation - Action - Result - Reflection

When preparing your examples, the S.A.R.R formula can help you structure your response.

- » Situation
  Begin by briefly describing the challenge, problem, or task.

- » Action
  Go on to describe what you did, how and why you did it.

- » Result
  Describe the outcome and how your actions affected the outcome or the people involved

- » Reflection
  Finally, you may offer a reflection. This can include what you learned from the experience and whether you would do anything differently in the future.

Consider the following example:

- » Situation:
  "I was in the staff room during my lunch break, and I could hear a lot of noise coming from inside the salon. I went to investigate and I was confronted by two, very bored, little girls. I could sense that their excitement was causing a disruption and inconvenience"

- » Action:
  "I immediately took the initiative and attempted to occupy them by offering to plait their hair while they made bracelets from some hair beads. Their eyes sparkled with excitement and I was able to keep them occupied for the remainder of their visit"

- » Result:
  "We had lots of fun and, while the calm was restored, the stylist was able to complete the clients' treatment"

- » Reflection:
  "I felt really pleased that with just a little extra effort, I had made such a big difference"

Follow up Questions

Although the S.A.R.R formula will eliminate the recruiters need to ask some follow up questions, there will always be areas that the recruiter wants to probe further into. So, it is important to have examples ready to back up any statements made.

Prepare to be asked:

- » What did you learn from the experience?

- » What specifically did you say?

- » How did you feel?

- » Would you do anything differently?

- » How did they react?

- » What other options did you consider?

- » Why did you decide to take the action that you did?

- » You mentioned ... Tell me more about that.

- » How did you retain your composure?

- » Can you give me an example of that?

- » Can you be more specific about ...?

In some circumstances, the recruiter may even interrupt your responses with supplementary questions. Take a look at the following example.

- » Candidate
  "Working in a creative environment with other highly skilled professionals, it was natural that we had the occasional clash of ideas."

- » Recruiter
  "Please can you elaborate further?"

- » Candidate
  "We would sometimes have a clash of ideas based around our individual preference towards certain products, styles, magazines or equipment. Although, any disagreements we did have were relatively minor and insignificant."

- » Recruiter
  "What would you consider minor and insignificant?"

- » Candidate
  "Our debates were never confrontational, and they never interfered with our work in any way. In fact, some disagreements were quite educational."

» Recruiter
"Educational?"

» Candidate
"Yes, some very interesting views emerged from these debates which sometimes resulted in people, including myself, having a slight change in perspective."

» Recruiter
"Can you tell me about a change you had in perspective following such a debate?"

Lack of relative experience

If you don't have any relative experience in a particular area, you need to be honest and say so, but don't just leave it there. Use the opportunity to remind the recruiters of the skills that you do have or explain how you would handle the situation if it arose.

If you have faced a similar situation, you could say "I can't remember ever being in that situation, however, I did face something slightly similar that I could tell you about?".

Customer
Focus

1

When have you gone out of your way for a customer?

Sample Response 1

Situation:
I had a client call into the store who was looking for a very specific style of fabric. She had visited several stores in and around the area but hadn't been successful in her search.

I could see that she was exhausted, but also very determined. She spoke with such sorrow in her voice that I actually began to feel sorry for the poor lady because I didn't have the fabric to sell her.

Action:
Not wanting to be the bearer of more bad news, I decided to offer my assistance. I spent several hours ringing around wholesalers, distributors and manufacturers trying to track down this particular fabric, when finally I struck gold with a small manufacturing plant.

Result:
Because the fabric was a special order, there was a small handling charge, but the customer received the fabric within a few days and was sure it was worth the expense and wait.

Sample Response 2

Situation:
I encountered a problem when one of my clients was unable to have a hair treatment carried out in her home because it was being renovated.

Action:
In an attempt to keep the client, I spoke to a contact I had within a local salon and was able to negotiate a small fee for use of the salon facilities.

Result:
This worked out really well because it was convenient for both myself and the client to travel to. Since then, I have negotiated similar deals with four other salons and have increased my customer base dramatically as a direct result.

2

Describe a time when your customer service could have been better?

Evaluation

Providing excellent customer service is vital, so you should be very cautious when providing negative examples.

You could take a modest approach and explain that you always strive to do better, or you could be honest with humble example.

Alternatively, you could attempt to avoid providing an example by explaining how you maintain your standards, and then proceed with an example of a time when you have demonstrated this capability.

Sample Response (Modest approach)

I take great pride in providing the best service I possibly can, but in doing so I increase my skills and can always see room for improvement.

Sample Response (No experience)

I take great pride in providing the best service I possibly can, and I never let my standards slip. Even during times of high pressure, I make an effort to remain courteous and helpful. I can honestly say that I have never received any negative feedback.

3

When have you solved a customer problem?

Evaluation

The recruiter wants to get an idea of how you apply your initiative and problem-solving skills to customer related issues. A good answer here will demonstrate that you always put in extra effort to provide good customer service and are not intimidated by difficult situations.

Sample Response

Situation:
I remember a client who came to me to have her hair extensions replaced. She had worn sewn in extensions for several months and was experiencing some discomfort from the attachments.

Action:
As I examined her hair, I was shocked to discover how much damage had been caused. Her roots had become severely matted and the tightness from the installed tracks had created spots of baldness.

I took a moment to analyse the situation, work out a strategy and then I set to work.

I spent several hours meticulously untangling every hair and removing every extension piece, The more I removed, the more I could see the scale of the damage that had been caused. Sadly, the client's hair was in very bad shape after the removal and the spots of baldness were very evident. Needless to say, I had a very emotional customer.

I applied a very deep conditioning protein treatment to the customers remaining locks and gave it a good trim. I then finished up with some fine and strategically placed fusion hair extensions to conceal the bald patches and create some much needed volume.

Result:
Following the treatment, the client looked fantastic and her smile was restored. Her hair soon returned to its former glory and she became a regular client of mine.

4 | When have you tended to an upset customer?

Sample Response

Situation:
I recently experienced a situation with a client who was having relationship problems. She was becoming increasingly emotional and I could sense that she was feeling very depressed.

Action:
Although I felt compassion for her situation, I knew that it was important for me not to get overly involved. So, I gave her chance to talk while I listened, and I tried to show empathy while remaining neutral and professional in my response.

Result:
Just being able to talk to someone who listened seemed to make her feel better. As she continued to speak, she appeared to have gained a deeper insight into her situation and actually began seeing things more positively. Consequently, she was able to calmly discuss her feelings with her partner and work through their problems. She later thanked me for listening.

Reflection:
From this experience, I learned that just listening can be providing good customer care.

5

Have you been confronted by an aggressive customer?

Sample Response

Situation:
Shortly after I began freelancing, I encountered a problem when an associate of mine tried to pressure me into a free service based on friendship.

Action:
I proceeded to offer her, what I considered to be, a reasonable discount, but she was not satisfied with my offer and proceeded to pressure me with emotional blackmail. I remained cordial, but became more assertive as I continued to refuse her demands.

Result:
Rather than accept the reasons for my decision, she became increasingly enraged, and even began to slander my service and friendship

Shocked at her over-reaction, and concerned about what might develop, I felt I had no option but to withdraw from the situation.

Reflection:
This experience was very challenging and certainly tested my patience. But I remained calm and, although this particular relationship never recovered, it was a learning experience that hasn't since been repeated.

6 | When have you had to say 'No' to a customer?

Sample Response

Situation:
I remember when a customer tried to return a pair of trainers to the store for a refund. Although the customer denied it, I could see that the shoes had clearly been worn.

Action:
I remained calm and polite as I suggested that the shoes could not be returned unless faulty or unused.

The customer become very aggressive and repeatedly threatened to contact our head office to complain about me if I didn't refund him immediately.

I remained assertive and suggested this would be the best course of action for him to take. I then proceeded to provide him with the full details of our complaints manager within the head office.

Result:
Realising defeat, the man stormed out of the shop and, to my knowledge, never did take the matter further.

7

When have you handled a customer complaint?

Evaluation

The recruiter wants to know that you are able to retain your composure and use your problem solving skills when dealing with a dissatisfied customer.

A good response will show that you never took the complaint personally, remained calm and courteous, and were able to create a satisfactory outcome for the customer.

Sample Response

Situation:
I remember when a customer complained about a meal they had purchased.

Because over two thirds of the entire course had been eaten, not only was it obvious that the complaint was insincere, but it was also against the restaurants policy to offer a refund under such circumstances.

The customer was becoming very enraged and threatened to write to the trading standards and newspapers if I did not give him a full refund.

Action:
I gave the customer my undivided attention while he vented his frustrations. Then, when he had finally calmed down, I calmly apologised for the dissatisfaction and proceeded to offer a meal deal voucher as a goodwill gesture.

Result:
The customer was clearly unhappy not to have received a refund, but he left the restaurant and, as suspected, never did take the matter any further.

8

When have you had to resolve a conflict between what the customer wanted and what you could realistically deliver?

Sample Response

Situation:
I remember a client who came to me for a colour treatment and restyle. She had used a virtual hairstyle software to create her ideal look and was beaming with excitement as she showed me the picture.

The style was notably very pretty, and it was clear that it was ideally suited to the client. Unfortunately, however, the client's hair had been through several perming and colour treatments, and the platinum blonde shade that she wanted just wasn't going to be possible at that time.

Action:
Knowing how excited the client was, I felt a little dejected as I proceeded to break this news to her. In the hope of relieving some of her obvious disappointment, I suggested a strand test to see if it would be possible to lift some of the colour without causing excessive damage. If the strand test were a success, we could perform a gradual transformation through the use of highlights.

Result:
Thankfully, the strand test was a success and the client, while naturally disappointed, was happy to go ahead with the gradual transformation. The result was striking,and the client was happy with the result.

Within nine months, the transformation was complete, and I had a very satisfied customer.

9 Describe a situation when the customer was wrong

Evaluation

Although the popular saying suggests otherwise, the customer isn't always right and the recruiter wants to know that you aren't Intimidated by such situations.

You will be assessed on how you approached the customer and went about dealing the situation. A good response will demonstrate your ability to use tact, and will show that you remained courteous throughout the experience.

Sample Response

Situation:
I remember a client who I had carried out a perming treatment for. After completing the treatment, I provided written instructions for how to care for her new perm which specifically instructed against washing the hair for at least 48 hours.

Unfortunately, the very next day the client washed her hair and the perm dropped out. The client was understandably very upset, but refused to accept that the perm had fallen out as a consequence of her own actions. She became very irate and started to slander my work and the salon.

Action:
When asked if she had followed the instructions, she denied being provided with any. I assured her that instructions were provided, and suggested she check her belongings.

Result:
Later that afternoon, the client returned to the salon holding onto the instruction sheet with a very embarrassed look on her face. She apologised profusely for her behaviour.

Reflection:
To avoid a repeat of this situation, I now provide clearer warnings within the written information sheet and back it up with verbal instructions.

10 Have you ever bent the rules for a customer?

Evaluation

There are situations where it is permissible to bend the rules, however, some airlines may view rule bending very negatively. So, no matter how trivial or well-intended, you may want to play it safe and declare that you have never gone against the rules.

If you do decide to provide an answer, you should show that you are able to keep balance between company policy and the interest of customers.

Sample Response

I have always abided by company policies and have never bent the rules. Bending the rules for one customer, will no doubt lead to a downward spiral . Either the customer will expect further rule bending, or other customers will catch on and expect the same treatment. It's just not a wise course of action to take.

Journal Notes

Communication
Competence

11 Tell me about a time when you failed to communicate effectively?

Sample Response (Modest Approach)

While I have certainly encountered communication challenges, I can honestly say that I have never yet completely failed in my ability to communicate. With some creativity, I have always found a way to overcome communication barriers.

Sample Response (Humble Example)

Situation:
Generally, I am a very efficient communicator, but I do recall when I experienced difficulty communicating with an OAP client.

Action:
The client was very hard of hearing, and I tried everything to communicate with her. I spoke slower, louder, used hand gestures and facial expressions, I even tried to write the information down, but without her glasses she was unable see my writing clearly.

Result:
Fortunately, I managed to locate a magnifying glass, which enabled the client to read my instructions, and everything worked out well in the end.

12 When have your communication skills made a difference to a situation or outcome?

Sample Response

Situation:
I remember a trainee apprentice we had in our department who never asked questions and refused all offers of help. Unfortunately, instead of trying to understand her reasons, everyone drew the conclusion that she was a know-it-all and vowed not to offer help in the future.

Action:
Concerned that her progress would suffer, I decided to offer my encouragement and support. It soon became evident from our conversation that she had excessively high expectations of herself and feared looking incompetent. I explained that it was okay to ask questions, and mistakes were expected. I even shared a few of my own early mishaps to lighten the mood.

Result:
Very quickly after that we saw a change in her behaviour. She began asking questions, she was more open to suggestions, and her skills improved immensely.

Reflection:
From this experience, I learnt that things are not always what they appear and we need to be more objective before making rash judgements.

13

Give an example of when you had to present complex information in a simplified manner in order to explain it to others

Evaluation

As cabin crew, you may be required to break down and convey complex information to customers. For example, if a passenger is afraid of flying, you may need to explain the technicalities of the flight, or if a passenger is hasn't grasped the use of emergency equipment and emergency procedures, you may need to break the information down further.

Your answer here should show that you are able to express knowledge in a clear and simple manner.

Sample Response

Situation:
I remember a client who was interested in having a colour treatment carried out. She was very inquisitive and asked numerous questions, so I could sense that she was concerned about the process and potential damage to her natural hair.

Action:
Not satisfied with a simple nontechnical version, I had to provide a detailed technical breakdown of the whole process. This involved describing the molecular structure of the hair, the effect colour particles have and how they bond to the structure.

Result:
Although I had to occasionally refer to training manuals to emphasise or clarify my point, overall the client was satisfied with my effort. As a direct result, she went ahead with the treatment and was very pleased with the outcome.

14 Have you ever had to overcome a language barrier?

Evaluation

As cabin crew, you will interact with a variety of people from a broad range of cultures and backgrounds. The ability to relate to others and adapt your communication style is, therefore, very important.

Sample Response

Situation:
During a trip to Africa, I became acquainted with a French lady. She understood my French, the little amount I knew, but she didn't really understand English. Unfortunately, the amount of French I knew wasn't enough to get me through a whole conversation, so I had to improvise.

Action:
I spoke French wherever possible and filled in the gaps with improvised sign language and facial expressions.

Result:
At first it was a little tricky trying to find imaginative ways to communicate, but over time I became much more proficient. I'm sure she was amused by my amateur efforts, but it worked out well and I came away with a new friend.

Reflection:
Now when I encounter this type of communication barrier, I am much more confident in my ability to cope.

Journal Notes

Team
Spirit

15 Tell me about a time that you had to work as part of a team

Sample Response

Situation:
There was a particular time that stands out for me because it was such an unusual occurrence.

It was a usual quiet Tuesday afternoon and only myself, the senior stylist, an apprentice, and the salon manager were on duty. To our surprise, it was as if someone started offering out free chocolate, as clients started to filter through the doors.

Action:
Despite the overwhelming rush, we showed great teamwork as we pulled together and shared our duties. Even our manager showed great team spirit as she got involved with the hair service.

Result:
As a result of our teamwork, and some free relaxing conditioning treatments, we managed to deliver an outstanding service. Every client went away completely satisfied.

16   When have you struggled to fit in?

Evaluation

With the constant rotation of crew, there will be some people that you don't immediately hit it off with. The recruiters want to know that you aren't intimidated by such difficulties and are able to move past any struggles.

Sample Response

Situation:
When I started working at Trina's Hair & Beauty, I was joining a very close-knit team who had been together for a number of years.

As a result of the number of trainees they had witnessed come and go over the years, they had become a little reluctant to accept new trainees.

I wouldn't say it was a struggle to fit in as such, but I certainly experienced some growing pains. With remarks such as 'if you are still here then' to contend with, I knew I had to prove myself.

Action:
To show that I was serious about the job, and was not a fly-by-night, I focused a lot of effort on learning my new job. At the same time, I continued to be friendly and respectful of my new colleagues while I made a conscious effort to get to know them.

Result:
As a result of my hard effort, It didn't take long for them to accept me and include me as part of their team. Naturally, I have become closer to some of my colleagues than with others, but we all got on and worked well as a team.

17 Have you ever experienced difficulties getting along with colleagues?

Evaluation

No matter how hard we try, or how likeable we are, there will always be someone that we don't hit it off with. To say otherwise, would not sound credible.

For the most part, this question is asked to determine your ability to get along with other people and manage adversity. The recruiters want to know that you don't allow conflict to interfere with work.

The best answer should show that you aren't intimidated or confrontational in such situations, but you put in the commitment necessary to build a respectful and healthy working relationship.

Sample Response

Situation:
I remember one co-worker in particular who flat out didn't like me. It didn't matter what I did or said, or whether I tried to avoid or befriend this person.

Action:
After a couple of days of subtle hostility, I decided to assert myself. I diplomatically explained that I acknowledged her dislike for me and I asked for input as to what I must do to create a professional relationship

Result:
Although we never became friends, we were able to maintain more cordial relations thereafter.

18 Tell us about a challenge you have faced with a colleague

Evaluation

Airlines have a constant rotation of crew on-board each aircraft and, especially within larger airlines, you may not work with the same crew members twice. As a result, it is guaranteed that you will encounter challenging situations with colleagues.

The recruiters want to know that you aren't intimidated by such colleagues or situations, and are prepared to use your initiative to diffuse or mediate as necessary to keep working relationships healthy.

Your answer should demonstrate your willingness to cooperate with others to resolve differences, improve relations, and manage conflicts. It should also display your ability to remain patient and positive in the face of adversity.

Sample Response

Situation:
I do remember one situation where two of my colleagues really didn't hit it off with one another. They were constantly quarrelling and everyone had lost patience with them, but no one wanted to get involved.

Action:
In the end, I decided to take the initiative and act as a sort of mediator to the situation. I was not their manager, so I had to be as tactful as I could so that I wouldn't upset anyone.

I started by explaining that I acknowledged their dislike for each other and then I drew upon the fact that they are both professionals and can, therefore, put aside their differences for the good of the team.

Result:
They had a pretty frank discussion and, although I can't say they ended up the best of friends, they did work out an effective strategy for working more productively together.

19 Tell me about a disagreement with a colleague

Evaluation

We all have disagreements with colleagues, but they should never get out of control or interfere with work.

You may choose to disclose the details of a conflict situation, but make sure it was minor and didn't interfere with work. Conversely, you may wish to play it safe and declare that while you have had disagreements, they were so minor that you don't really recall the exact details. You could then go on to reiterate some minor examples.

The recruiters want to know that you aren't intimidated by conflicts and have the ability to see things from another person's perspective. Your answer should demonstrate that you are prepared to use your initiative and interpersonal skills to improve relations with colleagues, even in cases where they cannot agree upon certain issues.

Sample Response

Introduction:
Working in a creative environment with other highly skilled professionals, it was natural that we had the occassional clash of ideas. Any disagreements we did have, however, were so relatively minor and insignificant that I would be hard pressed to recall the exact details.

Situation:
Our disagreements were usually as a result of our individual preference towards certain products, styles, magazines or equipment.

Action:
Our debates were never confrontational and they never interfered with our work in any way.

Result:
In fact, some very interesting views emerged from these debates which sometimes resulted in people, including myself, having a slight change in my perspective. So, they were often very educational.

20 Have you successfully worked with a difficult coworker?

Sample Response

Situation:
I remember one member of staff was always complaining. Nothing was ever good enough or couldn't possibly work. Everyone had lost patience with her but, because she was so incredibly sensitive, no one said anything.

Action:
I spent some time with her and tactfully told her that it appeared as if she was always putting our ideas down.

Result:
On hearing this feedback she was genuinely horrified at her own behaviour. She explained that she hadn't realised it had made everyone feel that way and agreed that from then on she would try to be more positive.

Very quickly after that we saw a change in her behaviour. She became more conscious of her own attitude and deliberately tried to be more considerate. From that point on, no one could have hoped for a more committed team member.

21 Have you ever worked with someone you disliked?

Evaluation

There will always be someone that we don't like and to try to convince the recruiter otherwise would not sound honest or credible.

For the most part, this question is asked to determine your ability to get along with other people and manage adversity. The recruiters want to know that you don't allow personal views cause conflict or interfere with work.

The best answer should show that you aren't intimidated or confrontational in such situations, but you put in the commitment necessary to build a respectful and healthy working relationship

Sample Response

Situation:
There was one colleague I worked with that I really found it difficult to get along with personally.

Action:
Instead of focusing on those things I didn't like, I put my personal views aside and focused on the skills she brought to the position.

Result:
My personal view of her never changed, and we never became friends, but we did work productively alongside each other without any problems.

22 Have you ever acted as a mentor to a coworker?

Evaluation

There may be times when you have to mentor new crew members and the recruiters are trying to assess your ability to lead and mentor your colleagues.

Sample Response

Situation:
I remember when one of our trainees was having problems understanding certain aspects of her course material, and I could see she was becoming increasingly frustrated and self critical.

Action:
Having witnessed her in action, I knew that she was a very bright and talented individual with no obvious lack of skill. So, I determined that her frustrations were probably the result of the pressure she was feeling about her approaching exam.

Concerned at the effect this pressure was having on her, and having experienced the same pressures myself, I decided to offer my support. To reinforce her understanding, I demonstrated some of the techniques she had been struggling with and showed her a few memory tips and tricks which had helped me through my exams.

Result:
My breakdown of the processes, along with the visual demonstration I provided, seemed to make the material much more understandable for her. In the days that followed, she seemed to have a new lease of life and was much more positive. Subsequently, she passed her exams with top grades.

Journal Notes

Initiative
And Adversity

23 What have you done that shows initiative?

Sample Response

Situation:
When I began working for my current employer, the inventory system was outdated and the storage room was very messy and disorganised.

Action:
I came in on my day off, cleaned up the mess, organised the store cupboards and catalogued it all on the new inventory forms.

Result:
Thereafter, when orders arrived it was easy to organise and retrieve.

Reflection:
If I'm able to do the task, instead of waiting for the job to be done, I simply do it.

24 Have you undertaken a course of study, on your own initiative, in order to improve your work performance?

Evaluation

Your answer here should show that you are committed to self-development and take the initiative when it comes to improving yourself and your efficiency.

Sample Response

Situation:
While at Trina's Hair Salon, we were experiencing a spectacular rise in demand for high fashion cuts. I had some creative cutting experience, but nothing that extended to the kind of advanced skill that was required for true high fashion cuts.

Action:
After some consideration, I decided that increasing my creative cutting skills would not only give the salon a competitive advantage, but it would also be a fantastic opportunity for me to move my skills to the next level. So, I took the initiative and, under my own funding, immediately enrolled onto a creative cutting course.

Result:
My new skills proved to be an instant success. Existing clients began recommending me to their friends, which resulted in a massive rise in clientele. Needless to say, my manager was very happy.

25 Describe an improvement that you personally initiated

Sample Response

Situation:
While travelling in India, I learnt the art of Indian head massage.

Action:
When I returned to work, I began using my new skill on clients while carrying out the shampoo.

Result:
My massages were becoming such a success, that my manager approached me to request that I train my colleagues. Naturally, I was honoured to oblige.

26 Describe a new idea or suggestion that you made to your supervisor

Evaluation
The recruiter wants to know that you aren't afraid to take the initiative and suggest improvements.

Sample Response

Situation:
When I was working at Trina's Hair Salon, I had noticed that a lot of our clients wore nail extensions.

Action:
Convinced that the service would be an improvement to our already successful salon, I carried out extensive independent research before presenting the idea to my manager.

Result:
After carrying out her own research, she liked the idea so much that she decided to go ahead with the new service. Within a couple of months, the service was up and running, and we experienced a dramatic increase in new clientele and revenue. I even got a small bonus in my pay packet for my involvement.

27 Tell me about a problem you encountered and the steps you took to overcome it

Evaluation

The recruiter will be assessing how well you cope with diverse situations, and how you use your judgment and initiative to solve problems.

In answering this question, you need to provide a concrete example of a problem you faced, and then Itemize the steps you took to solve the problem. Your answer should demonstrate a patient and positive attitude towards problem solving.

Sample Response

Situation:
Early in my freelancing career, I experienced several clients who turned up late to their appointments. Some even forgot about their appointments altogether. Rather than just simply being an inconvenience, it was wasting my time and money.

Action:
I considered my options and decided that the best solution would be to send out reminder cards a few days prior to client appointments. For the repeat offenders, I would enforce a late cancellation fee.

Result:
This decision drastically cut the number of late arrivers, and I have never since had a no-show.

28 Tell me about a problem that didn't work out

Evaluation

No matter how hard we try, there are some instances where a problem just doesn't work out. To say otherwise will not sound honest or credible.

In answering this question, you need to first ensure that the problem was a minor one which had no negative or lasting impact on the company, a colleague or a customer. Try to accentuate the positives and keep your answer specific. Itemize the steps you took to deal with the problem and make it clear that you learnt from the experience.

Sample Response

Situation:
Shortly after I began freelancing, my bank returned a client's cheque to me through lack of funds.

Action:
At first, I was sure it was a mistake caused through an oversight on the part of my client. I made a number of calls, left several messages and even attempted a visit to the clients home, all to no avail.

Several weeks passed and it was clear that I was chasing a lost cause. At this point, I had to decide whether to write off the debt and blacklist the client or visit the Citizens' Advice for advice on retrieving the funds.

Result:
After careful consideration of all the factors involved, I decided to write the debt off as a learning experience.

Reflection:
In hindsight, I realise it was a silly mistake that could easily have been avoided. I have never repeated this error since as I now wait for the funds to clear before carrying out a service.

29 Have you ever taken the initiative to solve a problem that was above your responsibilities?

Sample Response

Situation:
It had been quite an uneventful afternoon when, all of the sudden, in walked an obviously frantic customer.

From what I could understand, her laptop had contracted a virus while connected to the internet and the system now failed to respond to any commands.

Being a self-employed web designer, the customer was naturally very concerned about the potential loss of data, and earnings.

Unfortunately, while the laptop was still within warranty, it was beyond the companies scope and had to be sent to the manufacturer for restoration. My colleagues, while polite, but could only offer assistance as far as sending the laptop to the manufacturer.

Action:
I could sense the customer was becoming increasingly distressed and, having had previous training in system restoration, I was confident that I could at least safely extract the data from the hard drive.

After talking the customer through the procedure, she granted her permission and I proceeded.

Result:
After some 45 minutes of fiddling with wires and hard drives, the customer's data had been successfully, and safely, extracted. The customer gasped a big sigh of relief as we packaged the laptop off to the manufacturer for repair.

Several weeks later, my line manager received a letter from the customer complimenting my efforts.

Reflection:
I was really pleased that a little effort made such a big difference.

30

When have you made a bad decision?

Evaluation

We all make decisions that we regret, and to say otherwise will not sound honest or credible.

The recruiter will be assessing whether you have the character to admit and take responsibility for your mistake, whether your decision had a negative impact on customers or the company, and whether you learnt from this mistake?

In answering this question, you need to first ensure that the mistake was a minor one, which had no negative or lasting impact on the company, a colleague or a customer. Try to accentuate the positives and keep your answer specific. Itemize what you did and how you did it. Finally, you need to make it clear that you leant from the mistake and will be certain not to repeat it.

Sample Response

Situation:
Early in my freelance career, I was approached by a salesman who was promoting a protein conditioning system. He described the system as "The newest technology to emerge from years of research. Guaranteed to help heal, strengthen, and protect".

Although I was excited by the concept, I did have my concerns that the system sounded too good to be true. However, the salesman had all the official paperwork to back up his claims, and the literature was thorough and well presented. All these things, combined with the company's full money-back guarantee, made it appear to be a win-win situation, and a risk worth taking. So I invested.

Following my investment, I decided to test the system out on training heads before taking the system public. Unfortunately, several months of using the system passed with no obvious benefits.

Action:
Disappointed with the product, I decided to pursue the full money back guarantee, but the sales number was not recognised, and my letters were returned unopened. Even their website had mysteriously vanished. I soon came to the realisation that I had been taken in by an elaborate scam.

I contacted the Citizens Advice Bureau and Trading Standards, but there was little they could do to retrieve my funds.

Result:
Unfortunately, I never recovered my costs and had to put the mistake down to a learning experience.

Reflection:
Unfortunately, it really was my fault. I should have trusted my gut instinct and carried out thorough research before making my decision. It is a mistake I shall never repeat.

31

What was the biggest challenge you have faced?

Evaluation

In answering this question, you need to provide a concrete example of a challenge you faced, and then Itemize the steps you took to overcome that challenge.

Your answer should display a patient and positive attitude when challenging situations occur.

Sample Response

Situation:
To be honest, giving up smoking was the biggest challenge. I never thought I could do it, and I had made dozens of attempts that ended in failure.

Action:
Determined not to give in to my withdrawals, I decided I needed an incentive that would pull me through the tough times. Being sponsored for a worthy cause was the perfect solution.

Result:
With a good cause in mind, the following three months were easier than on previous occasions. Not only have I come out the other end a non-smoker, I also managed to raise £2464.00 for Childline.

Reflection:
Since I gave up smoking, I have gained so much personal insight, and I deal with potentially stressful situations at work so much more effectively now, I feel more energetic, more mentally alert and far calmer now than I ever did before.

Traditional
Questions

Tell me about yourself

"As you can see from my résumé, I currently work as a freelance hair consultant, and have worked in client-facing roles for the past eight years. During this time, I have worked my way up from a receptionist to a senior hair stylist, while simultaneously studying for my NVQ levels 1, 2 and 3.

Now, this brings me to why I am here today, interviewing with you.

I have always wanted to become cabin crew and, during the course of my career, I have been gradually mastering the skills needed to perform its tasks. I'm confident that the customer care and teamwork skills I have developed throughout the course of my career, combined with my friendly and positive nature, will complement your existing team and enable me to deliver the standard of service that passengers have come to expect from Fly High Airlines.

I'd now like to discuss how I might continue my success by joining your team."

Cabin Crew

What do you know about the job?

"I know that the service we see as passenger's form only a small portion of what actually goes on in the job. With safety being the primary concern, there are procedures and checks which must be constantly and consistently completed. Then, when things go wrong, cabin crew are there to take control. Moreover, it is a constant process of cleaning and preparation, paperwork and stock checks, tending to passenger comfort and being of service. Clearly the profession is a very demanding one, but it is also a very exciting and fulfilling one for the right person, which I do believe I am."

Why do you want to become cabin crew?

"As a child, I was fascinated by aircraft and always felt a buzz of excitement when planes flew overhead. This is where my passion for flying initially began, but it wasn't until I carried out a career suitability test at college that I really started to consider cabin crew as a serious future prospect. The test examined personal attributes, interests and skills, and the final result came back suggesting suitability for the occupation. I done some further research into the job and instantly agreed. This job is tailored to my personality, skills and experience and is one I will feel committed to. Moreover, it is one I am confident that I will be good at."

Do you think the role of cabin crew is glamorous?

"Having thoroughly researched the position, I am aware that the glamour associated with the role is rather superficial. Sure there are benefits of travel, and the crew certainly do make themselves appear glamorous, but the constant travelling between time zones, the long and tiring shifts, unpredictable schedules and irregular working patterns place tough demands on crew and make the job anything but glamorous."

What do you think are the advantages of this position?

"The randomness and variety of the different crew, passenger profiles, roster structure and destinations excite me greatly. They are unique elements that you just don't find in normal nine to five jobs. It's a job I will find rewarding in a number of ways."

Reveal your passion

An honest and passionate response to this question will surely set you apart. Think about it, why do you really want the job? Where did the desire come from? Was it a childhood dream, or was it sparked by another interest?

Avoid being generic

Getting paid to travel, stay in luxury hotels and lay on the beach are obvious advantages the recruiter wants to hear about.

What do you think are the disadvantages?

"The obvious disadvantages are the flight delays and cancellations that crew experience. While passengers also experience these issues, crew experience those far more often. This makes for very long and tiring shifts, irregular working patterns and unpredictable schedules.

Moreover, the regular crossing between different time zones can take its toll leading to jet lag and fatigue. Ultimately, though, these challenges are part of the job and, with some advance preparation, they can be managed to a certain degree."

What would you change about this position?

"By applying for this position, I have accepted everything that comes with it. I see no point in concerning myself about those things that cannot be changed."

What aspects of customer service are most important to our passengers?

"Passengers want to feel comfortable and looked after by the airline and crew. They want to be assured that crew will listen to and answer their questions, and will be friendly and polite in doing so. If crew are not approachable, passengers feel unwelcome and unsure."

What do you think contributes to passenger frustrations?

"Feeling tired from travelling can cause passengers to feel unusually frustrated. Add to this flight delays, long waiting times and space constrictions, and frustration naturally increases. If the passenger is then greeted by seemingly unwelcoming staff, their tension will certainly rise much further."

Why do you think some passengers vent their frustrations on cabin crew?

"In the first instance, cabin crew wear the airline's uniform. Thus, passengers consider them to be a representative of the airline. Moreover, the passengers spend more time with cabin crew than with any other member of the airline staff, so they simply become an easy target."

What contribution can you make to ensure passengers will fly with us again?

My customer service experience and friendly character style will enable me to deliver a superior standard of service which will make passengers feel welcome, valued and relaxed.

Avoid sounding naive

To deny the obvious drawbacks of the job will only make you sound naive and unprepared. So, be up front about the disadvantages and demonstrate that you have considered these carefully.

Note

The recruiters ask questions such as these because they want to gauge your level of understanding of the job and its responsibilities.

What qualities do you think a good cabin crew member should have?

"Passengers generally spend more time with the cabin crew than with any other members of the airline staff, so they have a vital role in giving a good impression of the airline as a whole. This means crew members need to have good communication and customer care skills, as well as a friendly and welcoming demeanour.

Because of the importance of safety, it is also important that they have the strength of character to cope with difficult people and situations, in a calm and objective manner.

These are all attributes I possess, and are the primary reason I would complement your existing team."

Why should we hire you instead of someone with cabin crew experience?

"Although I might not have cabin crew experience, I have the necessary skills to make an impressive start, and the willingness to learn and improve. Sometimes, employers do better when they hire people who don't have a great deal of repetitive experience. That way, they can train these employees in their methods and ways of doing the job. Training is much easier than untraining."

Why should we hire you for this position rather than another applicant?

"I can't tell you why you should hire me instead of another candidate but, I can tell you why you should hire me."

Why should we hire you?

"As you can see from my résumé, I have worked in client facing roles for the past eight years. So, I am certainly qualified to perform the diverse requirements of this role. Also, the fact that I have been promoted through the ranks is a clear testament to my abilities and the confidence my manager had in me.

More significantly, my character is tailored to the role. As you will have observed during the group assessments, I am a very welcoming and social individual who interacts well with others. I readily adapt to new people and environments, I am hard working and think fast on my feet.

I am confident that these aspects of my personality and experience will enable me to perform the job to the same high standard that exists currently."

Sell Yourself

This is the time to shine, so don't be modest. Consider the experience and character traits that are most relevant and transferable to the position and, for greater impact, explain how you have demonstrated these in the past.

Are you willing to start as a trainee?

"Yes, absolutely. This is a new area for me, and I believe in getting a good foundation in the basics before progressing. An entry level position will enable me to learn the position inside out, and will give me the opportunity to grow when I prove myself. I also have a great deal of knowledge and work experience, which I'm sure will contribute to my successful progression through training."

How do you feel about the probationary period?

"I can see no problem with a probationary period. I am a fast learner so it shouldn't take me long to prove myself."

How do you feel about working at Christmas, and other special occasions?

"Naturally, I would miss spending time with my friends and family, but my career is important to me and my family and friends respect and appreciate that fact. I am happy to make the sacrifice as necessary."

How do you feel about a formal dress code?

"I have always liked to dress formally and feel very comfortable wearing formal attire. I realise that a standard of dress is necessary in order to project a professional image to the passengers."

This is a long hours culture, is that a problem for you?

"I understand that this a demanding job, but I really do thrive on the challenge of this sort of work and have worked long hours in the past, so I am willing to work whatever hours are necessary to get the work done."

This position will involve relocating, how will you adjust to the different lifestyle?

"I realise that this position involves transfers, and I bore that in mind when I applied. I am fully aware of what to expect from the research I have done and would welcome the different lifestyle."

How do you feel about the routine tasks and irregular hours of this job?

"I accept that every role carries with it a certain amount of routine in order to get the job done. If my job involves repetitive work, it is my responsibility to carry it out to the best of my abilities. As for irregular hours I would expect to have an indication of my core hours, but will work the hours that are necessary in order to fulfil the requirements of the role."

Do you feel confident in your ability to handle this position?

"Yes, absolutely. I'm very confident in my abilities. I'm familiar with the basic job requirements and I learn quickly. It undoubtedly will take time and effort on my part, but I'm more than willing to devote that time and effort."

Do you feel ready for a more responsible position?

"Absolutely. I believe that eight years experience working closely with customers, has prepared me professionally and personally to move up to this role. My customer care and teamwork skills have been finely tuned over the years, and I know I am capable of greater achievements."

How will you cope with the change in environment?

"I welcome the challenge of learning about and adapting to a new environment, that's one of the reasons I'm seeking to make a career change right now. Any major change, while always containing some challenge is a chance to grow, learn, and advance."

The Airline

What do you know about our airline?

"Fly High Airlines began operating in 1980 with a single leased aircraft, serving just two destinations. The airline now serves 73 destinations in 48 countries worldwide and is rapidly expanding its route network, which is soon to include Bristol and Ohio.

As a testament to the airlines excellent standard of service, it has acquired over 250 international awards for customer service excellence, and is now one of the largest and popular airlines in the world."

Why do you want to work for us?

"My first passenger experience with Fly High Airlines was two years ago, on a flight from Dubai to Los Angeles. The service on board was so immaculate and welcoming, that I was instantly impressed. Following this experience I became a frequent flyer and, when I decided to apply for this position, I was in no doubt who I want to work for.

Once I started to research the airline further, I was pleased to discover that the airlines corporate culture holds true with my own values and beliefs. Specifically the open door policy and customer comfort initiatives. This discovery reinforced my desire further and confirmed my belief that I will indeed complement your existing team."

Have you ever flown with us?

"Yes, I have had the fortunate opportunity to fly with Fly High Airlines on several occasions now. With the attentive crew, outstanding meal service and comfortable seating, I always feel as though I am flying first class. I am now a frequent flyer and very happy customer. I now hope to join your team in providing this fantastic service."

How would you rate us against our competitors?

Example 1
"It's so difficult to be objective, and I really don't like to slight your competition."

Example 2
"My experiences with each of the airlines I have flown with have all been good, and I never had a problem or cause for complaint. An advantage of Fly High Airlines, however, is the attentiveness of the crew. They really take care of all their passengers and do everything to make the flight as pleasant as possible. I have always been made to feel welcome on board your flights."

Show your winning hand

This is where your research will pay off handsomely. So, demonstrate your enthusiasm by sharing knowledge that will reveal the effort you have taken to learn more about the airline and its operations.

Make an impact

To make the greatest impact, begin with a personal story, but close with a demonstration of your knowledge and fit for the airline. This will make you stand out as an informed and enthusiastic individual who has something more to offer.

Caution

Be careful in your comparison here. While you want to praise the airline, you should never slander other airlines in the process.

Do you think we have a good reputation?

"Absolutely! Through my own experience, I have encountered attentive and efficient crew, fantastic meals and comfortable seating. In researching the airline, it appears that others agree with these observations.

The variety of awards the airline has received over the years is a sure testament to its fantastic reputation."

Inject Humour

Pointing out the obvious difficulties in becoming cabin crew will inject a spark of humour and avoid getting into negative aspects of the service.

What is the worst thing you have heard about us?

"The worst thing I have heard about Fly High Airlines is that competition for jobs is fierce because it is such a terrific airline. Everything else I have heard, have been overly positive."

Is there anything you think we do badly?

"In conducting my research into the airline, I haven't come across anything to suggest that you are doing anything badly. In fact, I have discovered quite the opposite.

Plus, I am sure you wouldn't enjoy your current success and be receiving so many awards for excellence if you were doing anything really wrong."

How do you feel about working for a small airline?

"I have always valued the feeling of a small company. They haven't become large and impersonal and I like the potential for being involved in the growth of the airline."

How do you feel about working for a large airline?

"I welcome the opportunity to work in a large, developed and well known airline such as this. The resources and potential for advancement are not available in smaller airlines. I'd be proud to apply my skills and abilities to the excellence that flourishes here."

Have you applied to any other airlines?

"Although it is taking a bit of a risk, I haven't applied to other airlines because I am set on working for you. I wanted to see how my application went with you before I considered other options."

If another airline offered you a job, would you take it?

"Because I am set on making cabin crew my future career, if I did not get this job with you, then I would have to consider other airlines. However, Fly High Airlines are at the very top of my list and I would be naturally disappointed not to get the job with you."

Career History

Why did you leave your last job?

» No opportunities
"While I enjoyed working for my previous employer, and appreciate the skills I developed while I was there, I felt I was not being challenged enough in the job. After working my way up through the company, there were no further opportunities for advancement."

» Redundancy
"I survived the first layoffs, but unfortunately this one got me."

» Temporary position
"The job was only a temporary position which I took to broaden my experience."

Why were you fired?

» Incompatibility
"I was desperate for work and took the job without fully understanding the expectations. It turned out that my competencies were not a right match for the employer's needs so we agreed that it was time for me to move on to a position that would be more suitable. I certainly learnt a great deal from this experience, and it's not a mistake I will ever repeat."

» Personal reasons
"I had been going through a rough patch in my personal life which, unfortunately, upset my work life. It is regrettable and my circumstances have now changed, but I really wasn't in the position to avoid it at the time"

Why have you had so many jobs?

» Broaden experience
"I wanted to experience different jobs to broaden my knowledge, skills and experience. This has provided me with a very valuable and rounded skill set."

» Temporary positions
"Due to the lack of full time opportunities in my area, I was only able to secure short term contracts."

» Youth
In my youth, I was unsure about the direction I wanted to take in my career. I have matured a great deal since those days and am now interested in establishing myself into a long term opportunity.

Fired?

If you were dismissed from any position, you need to be honest and say so. However, you should be tactful in your answer and turn it into a positive learning experience.

Never:
» Badmouth previous employers, colleagues or bosses.
» Place blame
» Tell lies
» Reveal team incompatibility

Why were you unemployed for so long?

» Study
"I wanted to broaden my knowledge base, so I went back into full time study."

» Travel
"I wanted to experience the world before settling into a long term career. I am now well travelled and ready to commit."

» Youth
"In my youth, I felt confused about the direction I wanted my career to take. I am now much more mature and certain in my desired direction."

» Personal reasons
"Personal circumstances prohibited me from taking gainful employment, however, circumstances have now changed and I am ready to get back to work."

Note

It is better to say that you chose to take time off between jobs than it is to give the impression that you were unemployable.

Why did you stay with the same employer for so long?

"I was there for several years, but in a variety of different roles. The opportunities for growth were fantastic so it felt as though I was undergoing frequent changes without actually changing employer. I didn't see the need to move on."

Why have you decided to change professions at this stage of your career?

"This career turnaround hasn't come suddenly. I have always wanted to become cabin crew and have been gradually mastering the skills needed to perform its tasks. I have now reached a point in my life where I am prepared to make the career and lifestyle change. I want to take advantage of that opportunity while it is presented to me."

What do you like about your current job?

"Rather than pick out the little details of the routine work, here are three general things. First is customer satisfaction. Seeing a client's face glow with happiness when their hair is transformed gives me an intense feeling of pride. Second is the interaction I get with my colleagues and clients. Finally, I enjoy being creative and finding new ways to please the customer."

What do you dislike about your current job?

"I honestly can't think of any major dislikes. I don't think I'd be able to really excel if I weren't truly interested in the work, or if I were merely motivated by its financial rewards. I guess my answer will have to come under the category or nuisances.

The biggest nuisance is the paperwork. I realise the importance of documentation, and I cooperatively fill out the forms, but I'm always looking for efficiencies in that area that will get me out in front of the client where I belong."

Which particular aspect of your work do you find most frustrating?

"That's an interesting question because I am, generally speaking, a tolerant person. Slow periods can be sources of frustration, but at times like that I put more effort into advertising and establishing new clientele. That way, the slow periods don't last long."

Caution?

There will always be less than exciting aspects of a job, however, being critical about your job isn't going to create a positive impression. So, soften these aspects as much as possible and try to select minor examples, such as paperwork, lack of job security or opportunities for growth.

Character Traits

What are your best qualities?

"As you will have observed during the group assessments, I am a very welcoming and social individual who interacts well with others, and readily adapts to new people and environments. In fact, my previous supervisor also picked up on these attributes and often asked me to carry out the shampoo because she knew I would make the clients feel welcome and relaxed.

I am confident that these aspects of my character will enable me to perform the job to the same high standard that exists currently within the airline."

What is your greatest weakness?

» Perfectionist
  I tend to spend longer than necessary making sure that things are perfect, and sometimes get a little frustrated if I don't achieve excellence.

  I did learn early on in my career that this slows output but, on the other hand, without such attention to detail the consistency and accuracy of my work could be affected. It is a difficult balancing act but I am working on finding a more balanced approach.

» Paperwork
  "I realise the importance of paperwork, but I tend to procrastinate if I don't build it into my schedule. I'm always looking for efficiencies in that area that will get me out in front of the client where I belong."

Are you an introvert or extrovert?

"Actually, I would describe myself as an ambivert because I enjoy social interaction, but am equally happy to spend time alone in my own company."

What makes you stand out from the crowd?

"My friendly and positive nature certainly defines me as a person and makes me stand out from the crowd. I adopt a very optimistic view in every aspect of my life and refuse to allow external circumstances to negatively affect my state."

Back it up

To give your answer substance, back up your statement with examples of when you have demonstrated these qualities.

Be Selective

Avoid declaring any key competencies as a weakness. Use insignificant skills which can be made positive with a solution.

Be Unique

Trying to highlight too many positive traits will appear random and over the top. Pick just one or two predominant traits which make you unique.

If you had to characterise yourself in one sentence, what would you say?

"I am a friendly and approachable person, who is sincere and very optimistic about life."

Rate yourself on a scale from 1 to 10

"I would rate myself as an 8. I always give my best, but in doing so I increase my skills. I, therefore, always see room for improvement."

How would a friend describe you?

"My friends would describe me as sociable, cheerful and optimistic. They would also say I am someone who thinks fast on my feet and stays calm in adverse situations."

How would an enemy describe your character?

"I suppose they might say that I am tenacious because I don't give in without a struggle, but am realistic about my limits. They might say I am brave because I am prepared to confront issues when there is a need, but I weigh the consequences and don't act irresponsibly. And, maybe, driven because I push for what I want, but can back off when advisable to do so."

How have you changed in the last five years?

"I feel like I have matured rather than aged five years. The skills I have acquired and the qualities I have developed have changed me enormously, and I know there are parts of me that are still not being utilised half as effectively as they could be. My customer care and communication skills have definitely been improved, and I have a better ability to use my initiative and think on my feet."

Customer Focus

How would you define good customer service?

"Good customer service is about constantly and consistently meeting customer's expectations by providing a friendly, efficient and reliable service throughout the life of the service and/or product.

Excellent customer service is about exceeding customer's expectations by going beyond the call of duty. I believe that because no two customers are the same, they deserve to receive a service that is tailored to their individual needs. This is where a service moves beyond being just a satisfactory one, and becomes an excellent one."

What do you think constitutes poor customer service?

"Poor service is when customers are treated with disrespect and provided with a poor quality product and/or service by rude, ignorant and unhelpful staff."

Do you think the customer is always right?

"Whilst every customer is important, they are certainly not always right. Those who exhibit abusive behaviour, or do anything to compromise safety are straying beyond the boundary."

When have you witnessed good customer service?

"I remember when I visited a local restaurant for a luncheon. It had just turned 3pm on a Wednesday afternoon and, much to mine and the management's surprise, they were exceptionally busy with only three waiting staff on duty. Despite the overwhelming rush our waitress, Claire, was very polite and helpful. The staff showed great teamwork as they managed to pull together and deliver an outstanding service."

Note

In these two instances, the recruiters just want to gauge your understanding of good and bad customer service.

When have you witnessed poor customer service?

"I needed a particular material for a dress I was making. In most stores the salesperson would give me a quick 'no' before I finished explaining what I was looking for. I hadn't really noticed until I experienced the opposite service in another smaller fabric store."

What do you enjoy about providing customer care?

"The most enjoyable aspect I would have to say is that because I genuinely care about my client's satisfaction, it rewards me personally when I know that they are happy with the job I did. This, in turn, drives me to do better."

What do you dislike about providing customer care?

"Providing good customer care can be a challenge, and some people may view that negatively, but I view each challenge as an opportunity to develop and grow. So, because I am committed to developing myself, I welcome and enjoy the challenges of providing customer care. It is something I have become very good at."

What do you find most challenging about providing customer service?

"Providing customer service is a challenge in itself. Because people are unpredictable by their very nature, you have to always expect the unexpected and be prepared to go beyond the call of duty and deal with issues as they arrive."

Caution!

Sure there are elements of customer care which are less than desirable, but this will be the main focus of your job. Therefore, you will want to turn this question around and answer it in a positive way.

Team Spirit

How would you define teamwork?

"Teamwork is a group of people who work cooperatively together to achieve a common goal. They make a coordinated effort and each individual contributes their unique skills and ideas to the task."

Do you prefer to work alone or as part of a team?

"I am happy either way, and equally efficient at both. So, whether I prefer to work alone or in a team would depend on the best way to complete the job.

I do, however, have a preference towards team spirit. As well as the interaction, there is greater satisfaction when you share the joy of completing a task."

Are you a team player?

"Absolutely I am. As you will have observed during the group assessments, I interact well with others, and readily adapt to new people. I am a good listener, I respect other people's opinions and I can be relied on to contribute to the overall goal.

In fact, my previous supervisor used to say that my infectious optimism created excitement in other team members and resulted in a greater team effort and higher output."

What role do you assume in a team situation?

"I am whatever I need to be. If a situation comes up and someone needs to take charge, then I will. But if someone else has already taken charge and is solving it, I will follow their lead."

What do you enjoy about working as part of a team?

"There's nothing like being part of a great team where you can learn from the other members, bounce ideas off one another, and share achievements and rewards. There is a unique feeling of camaraderie that can never be experienced from working alone."

What do you least enjoy about working as part of a team?

"People not pulling their weight can be frustrating. However, I've noticed that such people simply lack enthusiasm or confidence, and that energetic and cheerful coworkers can often change that."

Note

Naturally, there will be problems in a team situation, however, put a positive spin on your answer.

What do you find most challenging about being part of a team?

"The most challenging aspect is inspiring and motivating other team members. Each has different needs and is motivated by different things."

Are you happy to be supervised by people who are younger than yourself?

"Absolutely. I don't consider age to be an important factor. What matters is a person's credibility, professionalism and competency."

Communication Competence

What is the importance of having good communication skills?

"The ability to speak clearly, listen actively and comprehend effectively is vital for our successful interaction with others, and continued growth."

How confident are you about addressing a group?

"I used to be nervous about speaking in front of a group, yet I found that preparation, practice and knowing my subject helped me overcome this, I now have no problem addressing a group."

Rate your communication skills on a scale of 1 to 10.

"I would rate myself as an 8. I always give my best, but in doing so I increase my skills. I, therefore, always see room for improvement."

Do you think your lack of language skills will affect your ability to perform the job?

"I admit my language skills are a little light, however, I am working on increasing my language fluency and, should I be offered the position, I will be sure to work on increasing my language abilities even further."

Hypothetical

Hypothetical questions present candidates with difficult real-life situations, where almost any answer can be challenged.

A good way to approach these questions is to consider the feelings of everyone involved, and think about the implications for your colleagues and the airline.

Prove to the recruiters that you would be proactive and do your best to resolve the situation using your own initiative, whilst remembering that you could ask for the help of the more experienced crew if necessary.

If you have followed these guidelines and are still challenged, the recruiter may be testing your ability to manage conflict or stress. Bear in mind that if you are not cabin crew yet, you cannot really be expected to know the best reply so do not be tricked into entering into an argument with the recruiter.

In either case it is important to remain calm and focused, and to demonstrate that, although you appreciate there are many aspects to each situation, you would always be trying to find acceptable solutions.

If you really can't think of a solution, you can simply say, "That is a new area for me so I am afraid I can't really answer that, but I enjoy acquiring new knowledge and I do learn quickly."

You are in flight at 30,000 feet. How would you handle a passenger if he became irate about his lost baggage?

"At 30,000 feet, there is not a lot you can do about the baggage, so the problem at hand is reassuring the passenger and avoiding further disruption.

First, I would try to manoeuvre the passenger somewhere more private where they can explain the situation. I would then apologise for the mishandling, and offer to assist on the ground by escorting him to the proper people who can help."

What would you do if the seat belt signs are on due to turbulence, but a passenger gets up to go to the toilet?

"Because of the importance of passenger safety, I would advise the passenger to wait until the seat belt signs have been turned off. If the passenger really cannot wait, I will follow the corporate policy for dealing with such a situation."

How would you handle a passenger who is intoxicated?

"I would not provide any more alcoholic beverages. I would encourage food, and offer a cup of tea or coffee. If the situation worsens beyond my control, I would inform my senior and seek assistance from the other crew members."

What would you do if a commercially important passenger complained about a crying child?

"I would apologise to the passenger and offer my assistance to the guardian of the child."

How would you deal with a passenger who is scared of flying?

"Being aware of what to expect, and just realising that a plane's wings are supposed to flex and move around gently in flight, can help relieve anxiety. Similarly, the collection of bumps and bangs that always accompany a flight can be made less fearsome if they are expected. So, I would try to comfort the passenger by talking them through the flight, and reassuring them of any strange noises they may hear.

I would advise them where I can be found, and show them the call bell. I would then check on them periodically throughout the flight."

How would you deal with a passenger who is not, right but believes he is right?

"I would explain the company's rules and policies to the passenger in a calm, professional and positive manner. Hopefully, this should clarify any misconceptions that the passenger may have."

How would you handle a colleague who is being rude or racist?

"I would act immediately to put a stop to any racist or rude behaviour by making it clear to the person that their behaviour is not acceptable. If he or she continues, I would then report it to proper authority."

If you spotted a colleague doing something unethical or illegal, what would you do?

"I would act immediately to put a stop to any unethical or illegal activity. I would try to document the details of the incident and try to collect any physical evidence. Then I would report it to my senior."

What would you do if you suspect that a passenger is suspicious or a high risk to passengers?

"I would keep watch before reporting to the senior any abnormal behaviour indicating a suspicious passenger."

What would you do and how would you react in a hijacking?

"I would remain calm, and follow the emergency guidelines and procedures."

How would you act in an emergency such as a crash landing?

"As soon as I get the warning that something is going to happen, I would get a plan together in my mind. I would stay calm and in control and follow the emergency guidelines and procedures."

What three items would you choose to have if trapped on a desert island?

"The three items I would have to have would be a medical kit containing various items such as medicines, water purification tablets, surgical blades, plasters and cotton wool. Second, I would have my survival kit containing essential items such as a compass, a striker and flint, torch, waterproof matches, a magnifying glass, and fish hooks and line. Third, a good survival guidebook."

If you were trapped on a desert island, what book would you want?

"I would have to have an SAS survival guide."

If you were going to Mars, what three items would you take?

"First, I would take a trained astronaut. Second, sufficient food for the journey and finally, enough fuel for the return trip."

Adverse

Have you stretched the truth today to gain a favourable outcome?

"Absolutely not. I haven't tried to be someone I am not, because I wouldn't want to get the job that way. To do so would be such a short term gain because eventually I would be found out."

How would you respond if we told you that you have been unsuccessful on this occasion?

"Naturally, I will be a disappointed if I do not secure this job with you because it is something I really want, I feel ready for it, and I have had plenty to contribute. However, I am not one to give up quickly. I will think about where I went wrong and how I could have done better, and I would then take steps towards strengthening my candidacy."

What would you say if I said your skills and experience were below the requirements of this job?

"I would ask what particular aspects of my skills and experience you felt were lacking and address each one of those areas with examples of where my skills and experiences do match your requirements. I would expect that after this discussion you would be left in no doubt about my ability to do this job."

Aren't you overqualified for this position?

"I wouldn't say that I am overqualified, but certainly fully qualified. With more than the minimal experience, I offer immediate returns on your investment. Don't you want a winner with the skill sets and attitudes to do just that?"

What question could I ask that would intimidate you?

"I can't think of any question that would intimidate me. This is probably the most intimidating question."

How would you rate me as a recruiter?

"First, I'd give you high marks for your people skills. You helped me feel at ease right away, which made it easier for me to answer the questions. I'd also rate you highly on the creativity of the questions, and their thoroughness. By probing me as carefully as you have, you've given me a better opportunity to secure this position. You've given me a complete picture of what to expect at Fly High Airlines, and it confirms my belief that this is where I want to work."

Caution!

Try not to be thrown off by the implied failure of these questions. The recruiters are simply testing your reaction and want to see what action you would take.

I'm not sure you are suitable for the position. Convince me.

"I am absolutely suitable. In fact, I am confident that I am perfect for this position.

You are looking for someone who is customer focused. Well, as you can see from my résumé, I have worked in client facing roles for eight years so have had plenty of experience dealing with the various aspects. I also run a successful business that relies on customer satisfaction. The fact that I am still in business, and have a solid and increasing client base, is a clear testament to my abilities.

Furthermore, you need someone who has a calm approach, and retains their composure in the face of adversity. Again, I have demonstrated this capability on several occasions throughout my career.

Beyond this, I have a friendly and optimistic character. I am hard working, I thrive on challenges and will always strive to deliver the highest standard of service to your passengers.

I am confident that my skills, experience and personal qualities will complement your existing team and allow me to make a positive contribution to the airline's ongoing success."

Do you work well under pressure?

"Absolutely. Because pressure is the result of a new challenge, I perceive pressure as an opportunity to develop and grow. The more challenges I experience, the better my skills become, and the less I feel the pressure of subsequent challenges. So, because I am committed to developing myself, I welcome the challenges of pressure."

How would I know you were under pressure?

"I disguise my pressure well, therefore, I would hope that it wouldn't be obvious enough to notice."

What types of people annoy you or try your patience?

"That's an interesting question, because I am a very tolerant person. However, there are instances where my patience is put to the test, but I am able to control myself and my emotions, so I never let my patience move beyond the testing stage."

Do you have difficulties tolerating people with different views than you?

"No. I recognise that everyone has their own views, and that they may not always correspond with my own. Differing views and personalities are what make us individual, so I don't let other people's views or interests affect how I feel about them."

How often do you lose your temper?

"I never lose my temper. I regard that sort of behaviour as counterproductive and inappropriate. By losing your temper, you cannot possibly resolve a problem. Even if you're completely right, losing your temper often destroys your ability to convince others of this."

What makes you angry or impatient?

"Anger to me means loss of control, and I'm not the kind of person who loses control. It is counterproductive and inappropriate, and doesn't gain anything of value.

When I feel stress building up, instead of getting angry or impatient, I take a deep breath and begin to focus on the positives. The results are quite dramatic, my whole demeanour changes very rapidly,"

How do you handle criticism?

"As long as the criticism is fair and constructive, I listen to it and remain gracious. I thank them for their candid feedback, express regret over the situation and modify my future behaviour accordingly."

Closing

So you do still wish us to consider you for this position?

"Absolutely! Having had this chance to meet you and learn more about the airline and position, I am even more eager than before. I am convinced that this is the opportunity I am seeking, and I know I can make a positive contribution."

Would you take this job if we offered it to you?

"Yes, definitely. I was eager as soon as I saw the job opening on your web site. More than that though, actually meeting potential colleagues and finding out more about the airline and the position has clarified still further what an exciting challenge it would be to work here."

When are you available to start if offered the position?

"I have the energy and enthusiasm to start straight away. All I need is a week's notice and I'm ready."

Where do you picture yourself in five years?

"I very much hope that I shall be with Fly High Airlines in five years time. By which time, I will have made a significant contribution to the airline, will have become an experienced senior member of the cabin crew team, and will be working on new ways to advance my career further."

If offered the job, how long will you stay with us?

"I'm approaching this job with a long term view. I hope to make enough of a contribution the airline, that I can move up through the ranks to become an experienced senior member of the cabin crew team."

Do you have any reservations about working here?

"I don't have any reservations at this point. I see this position as a fine opportunity, and the airline as one I would be proud to be an employee of."

Can we contact previous employers for references?

"Yes, absolutely. I'm confident that all my references will be favourable and will confirm what we've discussed here today."

Interviewing the Interviewer

This section of the interview is a real chance for you to shine and set yourself apart from all the other candidates. Therefore, it is a good idea to prepare one or two intelligent questions in advance.

The questions you ask, and how you ask them, say a lot about you, your motives, your depth of knowledge about the airline and the position itself.

Guidelines

The questions you ask should follow these guidelines:

» Don't ask questions that could be easily answered through your own research.

» Ask questions which demonstrate a genuine interest in and knowledge of the airline and the position.

» Demonstrate that you know just that little bit more than is required.

Question About Suitability

Asking recruiters to raise their concerns about your suitability will provide you with an opportunity to follow up and reassure the recruiter.

» Do you have any reservations about my ability to do this job?

» What do you foresee as possible obstacles or problems I might have?

» Is there anything else I need to do to maximise my chances of getting this job?

» How does my background compare with others you have interviewed?

» Is there anything else you'd like to know?

» What do you think are my strongest assets and possible weaknesses?

» Do you have any concerns that I need to clear up in order to be a considered candidate?

Questions About the Recruiter

Asking recruiters about their views and experience in the job or working with the airline will demonstrate your genuine interest and motives.

- » How did you find the transition in relocating to ...?
- » Why did you choose to work at ... airlines?
- » What is it about this airline that keeps you working here?
- » It sounds as if you really enjoy working here, what have you enjoyed most about working for ... airlines?

General Questions

- » How would you describe the company culture?
- » I feel my background and experience are a good fit for this position, and I am very interested. What is the next step?
- » Yes, when do I start?

No Questions

- » I did have plenty of questions, but we've covered them all during our discussions. I was particularly interested in ... but we've dealt with that thoroughly.
- » I had many questions, but you've answered them all you have been so helpful. I'm even more excited about this opportunity than when I applied.

Questions to Avoid

You should avoid asking questions such as those following as they will make you appear selfishly motivated.

- » How many day's holiday allowances will I receive?
- » What is the salary?
- » When will I receive a pay increase?
- » How many free flights will my family receive?
- » Can I request flights to ...?

Journal Notes

Part 6

Conclude

Follow Up
You're Hired!

Follow Up

Sending a Thank You Letter

Writing a follow up letter to express appreciation and thanks for the interview is a must. As well as showing good business etiquette, it also presents an opportunity to make one final positive impression before hiring decisions are made.

To make the most of this opportunity, it is important to cover the following key points:

» Show appreciation and thanks for the airline's interest in you

» Reiterate you interest in the position and airline

» Follow up with any additional requested information

» Address unresolved points

» Remind of your suitability for the role

Guidelines

» Letter or email
While emails are more convenient to send, they also risk being perceived as less personal. Traditional letters, on the other hand, are much more formal and yet they also give a personal touch. So, unless online channels have been the primary means of communication or a preference toward email has been specifically implied, I would suggest sending a traditional letter in standard business format.

» Typed or handwritten
Handwritten letters are very personal and should be reserved for short notes. A typed letter in standard business format will work well for a formal thank you letter.

» Express your enthusiasm
Be sure that the tone of the letter conveys your interest and enthusiasm for both the job and the airline. Reiterate your suitability and summarise your strong points as they relate to the job, but don't oversell yourself as you may appear desperate. Keep the letter focused and to the point.

» Address unresolved points
If necessary, you could use the opportunity to address any issues or questions that came up during the interview that you feel you did not fully answer. However, don't draw unnecessary attention to anything which may be perceived as negative and never apologise. Maintain a positive, confident tone.

Note:

If you met with more than one recruiter, consider extending the courtesy by sending them all thank you letters.

Retain Consistency

To retain consistency, your thank you letter should continue the theme and format used for your cover letter (See page 73). When viewed as an entire package, it will create a very professional and consistent image.

Timing

Plan to send out thank you letters within 24 hours following the interview. Emails can be sent that same evening so that it is in their inbox the following morning.

Proofread

Make sure you convey a professional image by being certain that it reads well, and is free from spelling mistakes and grammatical errors. If possible, have a trusted friend proofread it before you send it out.

Jane Doe

16 Any Road • Any Where
Any Town • AN8 9SE
United Kingdom
+44 (0)4587 875848 • Jane.Doe@Anymail.com

Attn: Ms Loren   25 February 2011
Fly High Airlines
23, Airport Road
London
SW9 0DD
UNITED KINGDOM

Dear Ms Loren

Thank you very much for providing time from your busy schedule to talk with me about the cabin crew position at Fly High Airlines. I truly appreciate your time and consideration in interviewing me.

I felt a wonderful rapport, not only with you, but with all the team members I met with. I am further convinced that I will compliment your team and make a positive contribution to the airline's ongoing success.

As you requested, I have enclosed a list of references whom you may contact to further confirm my prior work accomplishments.

I am very interested in working for you and look forward to hearing from you once the final decisions are made. Please feel free to contact me if you need any further information.

Thank you for your time and consideration.

Yours sincerely,

Jane Doe
Encl

Figure 16.   Thank You Letter Sample

What Happens Next?

Following the final interview, airlines aim to follow up with candidates within two to eight weeks. Those who are successful will receive a job offer from the recruitment department by email, telephone and/or letter within this time frame, while those who have been unsuccessful will usually receive a computer generated letter.

In the instance that no contact has been made within the timescale noted, it is typically because the airline is no longer considering the candidates application.

For those candidates who have been successful, you will be advised of the various pre joining clearance requirements. These may include:

» Preemployment medical test

» Reference checks

» Joining forms

Once the required steps of the process have been completed, the airline will make the necessary arrangements to deliver the employment contract and relevant documentation. You will also be given final clearance to resign from your current employer.

Note

In some cases, employment contracts are dispatched to candidates prior to the clearances being given. In this instance, do not resign from your current employment until you are formally advised to do so by the recruitment team.

Coping with Setbacks

It may seem counter intuitive to provide coping strategies for rejection in an interview guidance book, however, in an industry such as this where supply exceeds demand, rejection is an unfortunate outcome that some candidates will ultimately face.

So, rather than be crushed by this outcome, I have put together the following tips for coping with, learning from and moving forward following a setback.

Prepare
The popular saying 'Prepare for the worst, but hope for the best' certainly applies in interview scenarios. If we attend the interview with an open mind, our attitude will be more relaxed, we will be better prepared and our coping abilities will be greatly enhanced.

Assess
Faced with rejection, it can be easy to misplace blame on ourselves, others or on the general circumstances. But, if we are to learn and grow from our experience, we must be objective and logical in our assessment rather than making rash and unsubstantiated assumptions.

> " A rejection is nothing more than a necessary step in the pursuit of success.
>
> Bo Bennett

Firstly, we need to reflect on our own performance to establish any possible areas for improvement. We can then make adjustments as necessary and shift our focus to the next opportunity.

Firstly, we need to reflect on our own performance to establish any possible areas for improvement. In this assessment, we could ask:

- » Did I dress appropriately?
- » How did I sound?
- » Did I arrive on time?
- » Did I remember to smile?
- » Did I appear confident and relaxed?
- » Could my answers have been improved?
- » Did I maintain appropriate eye contact?
- » Did I establish rapport with the recruiter?

If this assessment identifies any weaknesses, we can make adjustments as necessary and shift our focus to the next opportunity.

Accept

Sometimes factors exist that are beyond our control and the unfortunate outcome may not have been directly influenced by our performance at all. In this instance, all we can do is accept the outcome and shift our focus to the next opportunity.

Be Positive

Whatever the reason for rejection, it is important to treat each setback as a learning experience. So, don't become obsessive or overly critical, keep an open mind and be open to change if necessary. By handling the setback in this way, we will move forward and succeed much more quickly.

No Feedback

Due to the sheer volume of applications that airlines receive, a no feedback policy has been introduced and adopted industry wide. While this policy is understandable, it can leave candidates feeling crushed and confused as they are left to wonder, where did I go wrong? Unfortunately, this policy is unlikely to change so we must be objective in assessing our own performance.

Be Objective

When assessing your performance, avoid being overly and unnecessarily critical. In order to gain the most benefit from this learning experience, it is important to remain objective.

Important!

Airlines have a policy which requires unsuccessful applicants to wait 6 or 12 months (depending on the airline) between re-applications.

> There are no failures - just experiences and your reactions to them.
>
> Tom Krause

You're Hired

So you've survived the assessment process and now you're hearing those magic words 'you're hired', congratulations. This is an exciting moment and you should be very proud of your achievement. Now indulge in the moment, share the excitement and engage in celebration with your family and friends before returning here to learn what happens next.

Conditional Offer

The initial offer of employment is often subject to candidates meeting certain conditions and preemployment checks, such as:

» Satisfactory references

» Criminal record check

» Medical clearance and drug screening

» Appropriate visa clearance

» Signed contract of employment

» Presentation of original academic and professional qualifications

If any of the conditions are not met, the offer of employment can be withdrawn by the airline. For this reason, it is important to hold back from handing in your notice to your current employer until you have met the conditions and a formal contract exists between you and the airline. A formal contract exists once you have accepted an unconditional offer and signed contracts have been exchanged.

Background Checks

Prior to commencing employment, the airline is likely to conduct extensive background checks, including:

References
Reference checks form an integral part of the recruitment process and employment will certainly be contingent on receiving these.

Typically, the contact information for two professional references will be required. However, in some instances, airlines may request details extending as far back as five years. While the depth of information required will also vary greatly, you can typically expect most airlines to be very thorough in their verification process. The details included on your résumé or application will certainly be explored.

Common questions include:

» Please confirm starting and ending employment dates for (...) at your company

» Why did (...) leave the company?

» What position did (...) hold?

» Please describe the job responsibilities

» Please describe (...) attendance level

» Please describe (...) biggest accomplishment while working within the company

» Please describe (...) strong and weak points

» Would you rehire (...) if the opportunity was presented?

» Do you feel (...) would be a good fit for this position of cabin crew?

» Is there anything I haven't asked that you would like to share?

When selecting potential referees, ensure you select those people who can attest to your capabilities, such as managers, supervisors or team leaders. Where these are unavailable second choices could include colleagues, customers and academic professors.

Criminal Record Check
Owing to the secure nature of working airside, airlines will request a valid Criminal Record Check (CRC) to be presented prior to the commencement of employment. This check is necessary to obtain an aircrew ID and airside pass.

The CRC will include details of:

» Previous criminal convictions

» Reprimands

» Cautions

» Warnings

If you have any unspent convictions, these will be included on the certificate

Pre-Brief

After you secure permission of your referees, provide him or her with a copy of your résumé. This will ensure a better match of information when the reference is written.

Verify

Verify the contact information of your referees before handing them on to the airline. Check the address, phone number and email address, along with the spelling of names and job titles.

Permission

Before you assume a past or current employer will serve as your reference, it is important to secure his or her permission in advance.

Note

Responsibility for obtaining a CRC is the responsibility of the candidate, as are the costs associated with its accrual.

Medical Exam

Prior to being offered an official contract of employment, you will be required to undergo a full medical examination.

Typically, it will be the candidates responsibility to have an independent examination carried out prior to commencement of employment. In some cases, the airline may arrange an additional examination with their own designated medical team.

The examination will generally consist of:

- » HIV/Aids Test
- » Drugs Screening
- » Haemoglobin
- » Chest x-ray
- » Cervical Smear Test
- » Audiogram
- » Ophthalmic Report
- » Certificate of Dental Health and Dental x-rays

You will also be required to be completely up to date on your vaccinations, including the following:

- » Polio
- » Diphtheria
- » Tetanus
- » Typhoid
- » Hepatitis A&B,
- » Rubella (females only)
- » Tuberculin Skin Test
- » BCG Vaccination

The following page includes sample medical examination guidelines for your reference.

FLY HIGH AIRLINES
PRE-EMPLOYMENT MEDICAL EXAMINATION

1.0   Introduction to the Medical

1.1   The primary aim of the medical is to ensure that the applicant does not suffer from any disease or disability that could suddenly render him/her unable to perform his/her assigned duties safely.

1.2   The medical comprises of three main areas:

» Physical and Mental Requirements
» Eye Sight Check
» Hearing Check

2.0   Physical and Mental Requirements

2.1   The applicant should have no established medical history or diagnosis of any of the following ailments:

» Psychiatric or psychological problems including depression
» Alcoholism
» Any personality disorder, particularly if severe enough to have resulted in self injury
» A mental abnormality, or neurosis of a significant degree
» Drug dependence (The applicant will be drug screened as a pre-employment requirement. Candidates should avoid taking any sleeping tablets or cold remedies in the week prior to this.)

2.2   The applicant shall have no established medical history or clinical diagnosis of any of the following:

» A progressive or non-progressive disease of the nervous system, the effects of which, are likely to interfere with the safe exercise of the applicants duties
» Epilepsy
» Any disturbance of consciousness without satisfactory medical explanation of cause
» Cases of head injury with sequelae that are likely to interfere with the safe exercise of the applicants duties

2.3   The applicant shall not possess any abnormality of the heart, congenital or acquired, which   is likely to interfere with the safe exercise of the applicant's duties. A history of proven myocardial infarction shall be disqualifying. Such commonly occurring conditions as respiratory arrhythmia (irregular rhythm of the heart), occasional extra systoles (or heart beats) which disappear on exercise, increase in pulse rate from excitement or exercise, or a slow pulse not associated with heart conduction disorders may be regarded as being within "normal" limits.

2.4   The Systolic and Diastolic blood pressures shall be within normal limits.

2.5   There shall be no significant functional or structure abnormality of the circulatory system.

2.6   There shall be no acute disability of the lungs or any active disease of the structure of the lungs, chest or lung cavities. Radiography will form a part of the initial chest examination.

Figure 17.   Sample Medical Guidelines - Page 1

2.7   Cases of asthma or breathing difficulties, including shortness of breath, or wheezing shall be assessed as unfit if the condition is causing symptoms. A history of asthma as a child is acceptable if the condition is in complete remission without the need for preventative medications.

2.8   Cases of active pulmonary tuberculosis shall be assessed as unfit. Cases of quiescent or healed lesions may be assessed as fit.

2.9   Cases of disabling disease with impairment of function of the gastrointestinal tract or its adnexa shall be assessed as unfit.

2.10   The applicant shall be required to be completely free from those hernias or ruptures that might give rise to incapacitating symptoms. Any results of disease or surgical intervention on any part of the digestive tract or its adnexa, liable to cause incapacity in flight or reduce ability to work as required by the airline, in particular any obstructions due to stricture or compression shall be assessed as unfit.

2.11   Cases of metabolic, nutritional or endocrine disorders (e.g. diabetes) likely to interfere with the safe exercise of the applicant's licence and rating privileges shall be assessed as unfit.

2.12   Cases of significant localised and generalised enlargement of the lymphatic glands and diseases of the blood shall be assessed as unfit, except in cases where accredited medical conclusion indicates that the condition indicates that the condition is not likely to affect the safe exercise of the applicant's duties.

3.0   Eye Sight Check

3.1   The following are the requirements for eye sight of Cabin Crew

   » Good Binocular Vision
   » Distant Visual Acuity, with correction by contact lenses (if necessary), to 6/9 (20/30) or better
   » Near Vision Acuity, with correction by contact lenses (if necessary), to read N5 at 30-50cm and N14 at 100cm
   » Currently, spectacles cannot be worn and so only contact lenses are acceptable for visual correction. These lenses should be suitable for long-term wear in the dry aircraft environment. Soft permeable lenses are preferable and those candidates who require hard lenses (e.g. keratoconus) are not suitable.

4.0   Hearing Check

4.1   The applicant, tested on a pure-tone audiometer at the first issue of silence, shall not have a hearing loss, in either ear separately, of more than 35dB at any of the frequencies 500, 1,000 or 2,000 Hz, or more than 50dB at 3,000 Hz. However an applicant with a hearing loss greater than the above may be declared fit provided that:

   » The applicant has a hearing performance in each ear separately equivalent to that of a normal person, against a background noise that will stimulate the masking properties of flight deck noise upon speech and beacon signals;
   and
   » The applicant has the ability to hear an average conversation voice in a quiet room using both ears, at a distance of 2 meters (6 feet) from the examiner, with the back turned to the examiner.

Figure 18.   Sample Medical Guidelines - Page 2

Contract of Employment

Once the conditions of employment have been met, an employment contract will be drawn up. Once signed and accepted by you, this document becomes formally binding and you can now safely give notice to your current employer.

This contract will detail:

» The job title and a brief job description

» The base location

» The terms of employment

» The starting date

» Details of training and induction period

Ab-Initio Training

Successful candidates will be required to attend an intensive training program lasting between four and eight weeks.

The program covers both the practical and theoretical aspects of the cabin service and is very intensive. You can expect non-stop action as you participate in mock aircraft evacuations, fight real fires and perform life saving CPR on training dummies.

There will be regular assessments on all subjects studied and graduation from the course is contingent on passing these. The pass marks for each module are stringent, so you need to dedicate plenty of revision time outside the classroom.

In the event of exam failure, you are typically permitted one re-sit. A subsequent failure of an exam would result in withdrawal from the course.

Following graduation, the first six months of flying duties are probationary, and are seen as a continuation of this initial training,. During this period, you will receive further on-board training and assessments.

Yearly assessments will then follow on from probation.

Note:

It is important to note that although a formal contract of employment now exists, the contract is still subject to your successful completion of the in house training program. This shouldn't be a problem, but it is worth bearing in mind.

Journal Notes

9 781908 300003